'How Unpleasant to Meet Mr Eliot!'

'How Unpleasant to Meet Mr Eliot!'

Victor Purcell's *The Sweeniad*

Introduced by
SHEILA SULLIVAN

London
GEORGE ALLEN & UNWIN
Boston   Sydney

Introduction © Sheila Sullivan, 1985
The Sweeniad © executors of the estate of Victor Purcell, 1957, 1985
This book is copyright under the Berne Convention.
No reproduction without permission. All rights reserved.

George Allen & Unwin (Publishers) Ltd,
40 Museum Street, London WC1A 1LU, UK

George Allen & Unwin (Publishers) Ltd,
Park Lane, Hemel Hempstead, Herts HP2 4TE, UK

Allen & Unwin, Inc.,
Fifty Cross Street, Winchester, Mass. 01890, USA

George Allen & Unwin Australia Pty Ltd,
8 Napier Street, North Sydney, NSW 2060, Australia

First published in 1957
this edition 1985

British Library Cataloguing in Publication Data

Purcell, Victor
  How unpleasant to meet Mr Eliot!
1. Eliot, T.S.—Criticism and interpretation
I. Title II. Buttle, Myra. The Sweeniad
821'.912   PS3509.L43Z/
ISBN 0-04-800034-5

Library of Congress Cataloging in Publication Data

Purcell, Victor, 1896-1965.
  How unpleasant to meet Mr Eliot.
Bibliography: p.
1. Eliot, T.S. (Thomas Stearns), 1888-1965—Parodies,
travesties, etc. I. Sullivan, Sheila P., 1927-
II. Title. III. Title: How unpleasant to meet Mister Eliot.
PR6031.U7S9 1984   821'.912   84-14612
ISBN 0-04-800034-5 (alk. paper)

Set in 12 on 14pt Bembo by Columns of Reading
and printed in Great Britain
by Billings and Sons Ltd, London and Worcester

CONTENTS

Editor's Note	page	ix
Editor's Introduction		1
The Sweeniad		45
Preface		46
Bibliography		113

EDITOR'S NOTE

The title of this edition is quoted from Eliot's poem 'Lines for|Cuscuscarawy and Mirza Murad Ali Beg'.

It is assumed that a critical apparatus of full notes and references to the text of *The Sweeniad* is not called for; many comments and glosses will be found in the course of the Introduction.

The dates given in the Introduction will lead the reader to the source of reference in the bibliography at the end; if more than one of the same author's works appeared in the same year, a single word of the title is included with the date. All references to Eliot's poems and plays may be found in the *Complete Poems and Plays*, London, 1969.

The editor most gratefully acknowledges the help of Dr Hugh Purcell, the son of the author, and of Dr Leslie Wayper, of Trinity College, Cambridge.

EDITOR'S INTRODUCTION

Animadversions on Eliot

THE angry cry of Myra Buttle ('My Rebuttal'), denouncing the works of T. S. Eliot, has been all but drowned by more sonorous voices, and her work has been out of print for many years. It is time she was allowed her voice again, to add her vigorous views to those of the varied band of critics who dislike Eliot's work. There has never been an organised anti-Eliot movement, with full hue and cry, but nor has there ever been a time, since the publication of *Prufrock and other Observations* in 1917, when voices were not raised against him. When *The Sweeniad* first appeared in 1957 a new wave of restiveness was stirring, and heartily Buttle plunged in. Apart from its intrinsic interest as a curiosity of criticism, *The Sweeniad* may be seen, in its idiosyncratic way, as an embodiment of almost all the recurring complaints about Eliot's work. Far from the light-hearted frivolity it may first appear, it is an impassioned and comprehensive attack on Eliot's position as a mandarin of the age.

According to her Preface, Myra Buttle speaks in the person of a very ordinary shop-girl; healthy, busy, and surprisingly ready with references to Yeats, Graves, Empson, the Styx, and the date of 'The Waste Land'. The argument rather than the obscurity of modern poetry depresses her so much she is kept awake at night worrying about it. Then she has a dream about how modern poetry went wrong, and with a defiant apology she writes it down in her 'plain consumer's words'. So *The*

Sweeniad came into being, to take its place among the various books, essays and poems which abuse, deprecate, or parody Old Possum.

Myra Buttle was the name chosen for his works of parody and satire by Victor Purcell, an energetic and inquiring man, of broad interests and robust views, who led an unusually varied life. He was born in 1896, and fought with the Green Howards in France in the First World War – an experience which, he felt, sharply divided him and his comrades from those who, like Eliot and D. H. Lawrence, did not fight. His semi-autobiographical novel, *The Further Side of No-Man's-Land*, on life in the trenches and later as a prisoner in Germany, appeared in 1929, the same year in which he published *The Spirit of Chinese Poetry*. In 1921 he joined the Malayan Civil Service, and worked in colonial administration for over twenty years, making himself, by reading and travel and energetic application, an expert in Asiatic languages and history, especially those of China. In the Second World War he became a colonel, and from 1946 to 1948 served as Consultant on Asia and the Far East with the United Nations. Meanwhile he had published in 1944 a long and highly ambitious poem, *Cadmus: the Poet and the World*. From 1949 until his death in 1965 he was a university lecturer in history at Cambridge, specialising in the Far East. His long list of publications on history, linguistics, poetry and travel include several important works on the modern history of China, and in 1965 his autobiographical *Memoirs of a Malayan Official*. After *The Sweeniad* he published two further long satiric squibs, in mixed verse and prose: *Toynbee in Elysium*

(1959), directed against the ideas and influence of Toynbee: and *The Bitches' Brew, or the Plot against Bertrand Russell* (1960), in defence of the rationalism of Russell. Something of his wide range of abilities and interests is reflected in his two doctorates and the award of the CMG. Even these, however, do not reflect the ambition he nursed as a young man, and described in his *Memoirs*, to write ten lines of memorable verse, or failing that an enduring work of history.

It would be difficult to make out a case for *Cadmus* as a successful poem, yet it is deeply interesting, when we come to consider the attack on Eliot in *The Sweeniad*, as a pointer to what the author supposed poetry should be. *Cadmus* is a long work of vast scope, describing in ten cantos of complex stanzas, rhyming couplets, quatrains, blank and free verse the geological creation, the beginnings of life, and the long development of music and poetry. The origins of music and rhythm are found in man, and are seen to reflect the rhythmic structure of the universe. The clear stream of literature is traced from classical times through the Renaissance to nineteenth-century England, when after the death of the Romantics it became choked and wandered astray. But the spirit of beauty is indestructible, the poet claims, and remains so through all vicissitudes, including the horror and ugliness of the modern age and its misguided poetry. Though often ingenious and sometimes skilful, *Cadmus* is wholly derivative in form and language, with much emphasis on a dense Miltonic vocabulary, leaden rhyming couplets ('The jarring undertones of private aim / Confused the concord of the unitary frame') and lyric interludes verging on self-parody ('The snow-white lambs / Desert their dams / And gambol gaily on the lea'). The poem is highly revealing of the theories and beliefs which underlie much of Purcell's antagonism to Eliot, and implied in it are most of the objections he was later to express in *The Sweeniad*.

The Sweeniad was written rapidly in 1956 and privately printed the next year by the Broadwater Press of Welwyn Garden City, and the Sagamore Press, New York. Purcell's friend, Dr Leslie Wayper, believes the author made no attempt to have it published commercially, but by a process no longer discoverable, because the records have been lost, it was published by Secker & Warburg in 1958. It does not seem to have been widely noticed, but in June 1958 *The Times Literary Supplement* gave it part of a leader devoted to the art of parody. There was, it considered, some good parody in *The Sweeniad*, but the work consisted chiefly of burlesque and invective. It was 'a brilliant firework display', but altogether too derogatory for the gentle art of parody, and 'likely to leave Mr Eliot's withers unwrung'. Edmund Wilson also reviewed it with interest, and suggested that Purcell's failure as a serious poet had helped him towards his skill in pastiche (1958). Although the *Literary Supplement* clearly knew it was the work of a Cambridge don, it had been published anonymously – not, Dr Wayper believes, because Purcell lacked confidence but because he thought it might do better anonymously than if it came openly from the pen of a Cambridge historian. In spite of the echo in the name, there are no hints that the author knew of Roy Campbell's *Georgiad* (1931), or of Campbell's contemptuous name for the 'cerberus-hyena' of MacNeice, Spender, Auden and Day-Lewis as the 'MacSpaundy' poets. There is, however, evidence that Purcell had read Yvor Winters's attack on Eliot in *The Anatomy of Nonsense* (1943); and many echoes to suggest that he also knew the more intemperate work of R. H. Robbins, *The T. S. Eliot Myth* (1951).

Rather more than half *The Sweeniad* is in verse of various kinds, including blank verse, free verse, quatrains, and elaborate stanzas. Other large sections consist of straightforward observation and debate, written in polemical and often pugnacious prose. Sometimes the tone is ironic, sometimes heavily sarcastic, and sometimes merely irascible. Much of the work is clearly intended as parody, and although this occasionally loses its edge, and becomes mere imitation, much of it is adroit. The longest parody is of part of 'The Waste Land', here entitled 'The Vacant Mind'; but Dr Purcell is never one for modest shrinking, and he also parodies, imitates, or incorporates Milton, Shelley, Browning, Kipling, Graves, and many others among the great. Aptly following the method of Eliot himself, he sprays quotations liberally, borrowed from the ancient world to the present day. Sometimes the arrangement of these is highly skilful, as in the Chorus 'Ah, what avails the sceptred race?', where lines from Landor, Goldsmith, Eliot, T. O. Mordaunt and Browning are neatly carpentered into five quatrains.

The work is divided into three unequal parts: 'The Ghost Theatre', in which is expressed a general antagonism to modern poetry; 'Sweeney in Articulo', the much longer main section, which contains 'The

Vacant Mind'; and 'The Awakening', which forms a short conclusion. The entire work, set in the form of Myra Buttle's dream, takes place in a ghostly limbo where voices and choruses speak from the gloom and are often ill defined. The parodies and debates are loosely arranged, though not quite as loosely as the author himself suggests – 'No acts, no scenes, no plots, no choreography / No decor, theme, nor any definite geography'. For the first section of the work the chief protagonists are the Narrator, who represents the views of Buttle; a Voice, which speaks many of the verses and parodies, and is antagonistic to Sweeney; Sweeney himself; and a Chorus. In the second and main section the Narrator and the Voice arrange a critical forum in the shape of a Papal Congregation, whose task is to permit the public to decide whether or not Sweeney is worthy of the elevation he enjoys. A Postulator is appointed to put the case for Sweeney, a Devil's Advocate to put the case against, and the Narrator will stand in as the 'Pope'. Heated engagement in this debate sustains the long central section of the work. In the brief conclusion, 'The Awakening', Buttle urges a revolution by all true lovers of poetry, who will repudiate 'the tyrant clique', renew our tongue, and once again establish the reign of Harmony and Melody.

What emerge as Purcell's chief targets, and how precisely have they been hit? As a general theme, it is at once made clear that he dislikes and disapproves of both modern poetry and much nineteenth-century poetry as well. The greater part of 'The Ghost Theatre' – the first section of *The Sweeniad* – is taken up with a denunciation of the loss of rhythm and melody, the intrusion of a new scientific vocabulary, and the spirit of scientific reductionism. Density and obfuscation are satirised, modern life deplored, Freud castigated, and the prostitution of modern art decried.

With the introduction of Sweeney himself, with his 'frigid stare as cold as any cod', the attack narrows, and concentrates on his own work. Although there are various minor thrusts and forays, Purcell's chief offensive from that point on is directed against Eliot's Christian orthodoxy; the pessimism, elitism, and discordancy of his poetry; the presumption and misjudgements of his criticism; and his social and political beliefs. Of all Purcell's objections, his dislike of Eliot's Anglican clericalism is among the fiercest. In a neat turning of Eliot's poem 'The Hippopotamus', the Chorus 'Wrapped in the old miasmal mist' expresses a highly ironic view of the Christian mystery. The few conciliatory murmurs Purcell makes towards work earlier than 'The Waste Land' arise largely from the fact that these do not display a Christian bias. Eliot sees salvation from the moral and cultural breakdown of the modern world only through the supreme rule of the Church, whose business it is to interfere with the world, and to take the lead in speaking on moral affairs and on the conduct of domestic and foreign policy. The power of the sacerdotal caste must be felt throughout social and educational thought. The Postulator with ironic approval quotes Eliot's view that education must be fundamentally religious; that religious tests should be reintroduced for the universities; that 'the headlong rush to be educated' is to be deprecated; and that in the main only the wealthy and well-born should be taught, since 'to be educated above one's station leads to unhappiness and social instability'.[1]

In the mid-fifties, when Purcell wrote *The Sweeniad*, there was, he believed, an ominous religious revival under way. Humanist and rationalist views were abused, the churches were full – and Eliot was one of the leaders of this resurgence. Related to his belief in the necesary rule of the Church was Eliot's abiding attachment to a vision of pre-Renaissance Europe. This period seemed appalling to Purcell, and several times he returns to the attack. The muddled Aristotelianism of Aquinas, the damnation of unbaptised infants, the restitution of the Inquisition and of poverty and disease would all be a part, he felt, of Eliot's City of God. The influence of these beliefs on literature was dire, not least in that all literary critics now belonged to a right-wing establishment of the arts. Eliot's own standards of judgement were theological rather than literary, he and his fellows dealt in grace and sin instead of good and evil, and 'the mundo-Heavenly establishment' had gone far beyond its jurisdiction in seeking haloes rather than bays for its sons. Eliot's own contribution had been above all to offer the poetry and drama of purgation, damnation, and beatitude. The Negative Way of St John of the Cross, by which the soul to achieve salvation rejects the love of created things, is a philosophy Purcell seems particularly to have disliked. The idea of

---

[1] Most of Eliot's views on social and religious matters are to be found in *Thoughts after Lambeth* (1931); *After Strange Gods* (1934); *The Idea of a Christian Society* (1939); and *Notes towards a Definition of Culture* (1948).

renunciation as a creative act, by which the soul may be freed for rebirth, was of immense importance to Eliot, and it has recently been revealingly traced through his work by E. K. Hay (1982). It is not, however, a concept that appealed to the author of *The Sweeniad*.

Eliot's overpowering reputation had been achieved, Purcell felt, by a kind of secret conspiracy in which the literary, clerical, and political powers had all allied. The charge is repeated often: 'His cult is authorised in person or in proxy / By all the cardinals and priests, the ruling laity, and the acolytes of orthodoxy.' And again, Sweeney's reputation 'for reasons quite unconnected with his poetry, has been inflated altogether beyond his merits until even the most sceptical of critics feels constrained to speak of him with bated breath and down his nose'. Purcell was not the first to complain of this conspiracy of orthodoxy. As we shall see later, the strictures of R. H. Robbins on the subject of 'the affinity and gratitude of the Right' were equally severe (1951). And Yvor Winters complains that 'any attempt to analyze the defects of modern poetry in the light of civilized standards is accepted merely as evidence that the critic is not of the elect' (1943). Whether Purcell had read these authors or not, his own view of the matter was very definite and very angry.

His sympathy with the humanist and humanitarian view become very plain. He was outraged at the abuse suffered by the BBC when Mrs Knight made her broadcasts on Humanism in the mid-fifties; and no doubt held in contempt Eliot's view that 'a spirit of excessive tolerance is to be deprecated' (1934).

Purcell sketches, through the words of the 'Pope', his own vision of humanist man as enlightened, humane, tolerant, virile, zestful and humorous – everything which, in his opinion, Sweeney is not.

Contributing to what he sees as a pall of religious and moral gloom is Purcell's conviction that Eliot's poetry is fundamentally against life, which is to say that fertility and healthy sex have no part in it. In all the poems in which it is presented, sex is shown to be arid, bleakly lustful, or merely disgusting, while celibacy is raised to the highest spiritual value. The Chorus on castration, 'The lion and the unicorn', celebrates with bitter irony the triumph of sterility; and in Purcell's view the vegetation myth of the Fisher King has been inverted in such a way that it represents only barren despair.

Allied to this rejection, Purcell believes, is Eliot's general air of disillusion with the world. This pessimism he vehemently rejects. At no stage does he concede that noble qualities may be revealed also by their opposites. Myra Buttle's first and major worry, expressed in her Preface, is that 'The underlying message of the "Main Stream" poets seems to be that life is a sorry business'. According to the Postulator, the war resulted in universal disillusion, breaking the traditions of the past and bringing with it a cultural void, social decay, and a catastrophic decline in faith. From this moral bankruptcy the only way out was in the re-establishment of the Christian Church and faith. To have any meaning, life must be a preparation for death, for without that significance it can be only futile and bestial. Purcell appears to ignore the symbols of hope – the rose, wind, birds, water –

which are not negligible in Eliot's poetry. His vigorous objection to pessimism is further expressed by the Devil's Advocate, who asserts that it was the tragedy of slaughter, and not disorder and disillusion, which created the post-war crisis – if crisis there was. Humane social reforms were begun, and the young men still alive were filled not with despair but with an eager desire to build a better life. Eliot's attitude in 'The Waste Land' represented, in fact, that of only a fraction of his fellow citizens – a view shared by Spender (1975), Forster (1936), and others. Purcell clearly holds with those critics, who form the large majority, that the end of 'The Waste Land' offers no hope.

Other general problems of Eliot's thought and belief come in for recurrent attack. Purcell finds an air of condescension in Eliot's view of ordinary working people, whom he appears to despise ('the damp souls of housemaids'), and of whom he appears to have no accurate knowledge; the labourers in 'The Vault', Purcell asserts, are no more convincing than Lil and her friend in 'The Vacant Mind'. As for the Jews, when Eliot writes about them 'he spits like a cheetah'. His ethical attitude to literature and the dry self-importance of his manner are also made matters of strong objection.

So much for Eliot's beliefs and attitudes. When Purcell comes to reflect on the manner and quality of his work, obscurity – the old cry of Eliot's enemies – is a theme to which he frequently returns. Although Buttle declares in her Preface that it is the 'argument' rather than the 'obscurity' of modern poetry that depresses her, *The Sweeniad* is much concerned with meaning and obscurity. A good poem is now:

> The product of a highly specialised technique
> Of which the hierophants alone can speak
> By virtue of their rubrics, amended once a week,
> And issued secretly in Hittite and in Greek.

Speaking of 'The Vacant Mind', the Postulator notes with pained astonishment that there have been complaints on all sides of its obscurity, and later the Devil's Advocate accuses Sweeney of being 'deliberately obscure'. He is 'our greatest poet-obscurantist' and critics may interpret his poems as they will, 'each one's version of the sense / In equal keeping with the evidence'. Thus, says Buttle, the true meaning is impossible to come by. Purcell would have had no time, if he knew of it, for Helen Gardner's assertion that no one has any right to complain of a poet's being difficult (1949); or for Derek Traversi's admiration for Eliot's refusal to simplify (1976). Mockingly Buttle quotes from Eliot's prose: 'The more seasoned reader does not bother about understanding – not, at least, at first'; and goes on to object that all great poems of the past, including 'Jabberwocky', have *said* something as well as *been* something.

Purcell is greatly irked by what he sees as the elitist nature of Eliot's writing. The intellect and learning which he believes are demanded of the reader, and the arrogance of the appeal to the literary 'in' set, are highly distasteful to him. Eliot's use of allusion and quotation is a frequent target. Approvingly the Postulator quotes Eliot's line 'The immature poet imitates; the mature poet steals', then neatly adds his own gloss, 'but the artful poet learns to cover up his tracks'. In 'The Vacant Mind' full ironic use is made of this technique of Sweeney's, with much apt parody and quotation, including a resourceful substitution of Eliot's quotations from Webster and Baudelaire by lines from Fitzgerald and Shelley:

> I sometimes think there never blows so red
> The Rose as where some buried Caesar bled.
> If Winter comes can Spring be far behind?

And the praise of the Postulator knows no bounds when he comes to describe 'The Bloodbath of the Mass' ('Ash Wednesday') as a magnificent tract, some ninety per cent of which is constructed of borrowings from the liturgy.

Buttle castigates all modern poets for their scorn of harmony and melody, and sees Sweeney as the leader of this disastrous cult. The singers are all gone to Elysium, the poets caw, and all we are now left with is ditties of no tone. Employing the new vocabulary of science, modern poets need not fear 'to make cacophony' for science has no ear. To produce acceptable work the modern poet must be insulated from all that is beautiful, harmonious or inspiring – it is interesting here to remember Purcell's *Cadmus*. The splendidly quotable lines of the poets of past centuries, from Shakespeare to Shelley, are frequently displayed to show what has been lost. On the knotty subject of 'beauty' and 'greatness' Buttle finds no problem. The Devil's Advocate permits Sweeney a place as a minor poet, with some skill in scholarship and technique; but, because the modern poet is insulated from the stimulus of the imagination, the poetry of its great leader is suitable only for 'communicant parishioners'. Universal Poesy died with the Romantics, and in the thin atmosphere breathed by the 'moderns' greatness is not possible. As we might deduce from *Cadmus*, 'greatness' to Purcell seems to be largely equated with the more pastoral or sonorous passages of the poets who wrote between the sixteenth and early nineteenth centuries.

As to Sweeney's prose criticism, the words of praise delivered by the Postulator are all too clearly ironic. Here, he pronounces, Sweeney created yet another revolution. With commendable courage, he set out to follow Johnson and Arnold in a great re-ordering of poetry, placing Dante above Shakespeare, displacing Milton, Burns, Shelley, Blake and others to a lower order, and elevating Johnson as a poet 'of the highest calibre'. Now that the poets have been re-ordered, says the Postulator proudly, all the textbooks must be rewritten. The Postulator's description of Sweeney's amazing discovery of 'the demonstrative deductive nominative', which has revolutionised the modern critical approach, indicates Purcell's scorn for such critical ingenuities.

These are the main thrusts of Purcell's attack, covering both Eliot's beliefs and his writing. What they reveal of Purcell's own stance is of some interest. The moral position from which he fires his broadside is clearly that of a committed humanist, and many of his objections arise from this commitment. The influence of the Church, he believes, has been only for ill, and those who accept its rule are doing mankind a disservice. He is appalled at the hankering of Eliot, and like-minded Chesterbellocians, for the Middle Ages, which he regards as a time of cruel bigotry and rampant disease. Eliot's puritanical rejection of pleasure and the senses, and his increasing insistence throughout his work on the virtues of the Negative Way, Purcell finds unacceptable. His own very opposite philosophy embraces unquenchable hope for the future, enjoyment of the active life, and delight in the pleasures of the senses. The sketch towards the end of the work of the kind of man Sweeney was not, reflects Purcell's admiration for humour, compassion, and tolerance (although he did not manage to extend much of this last to Sweeney).

On the subject of literature, Purcell was combative in his crusading zeal, and totally unafraid of offending the literary establishment he found so misguided and corrupt. According to his own lights, he was clearly a passionate lover of poetry, at least of the poetry written up to about 1830. Shelley is cited in *The Sweeniad* even more often than Shakespeare, and clearly the Romantics were among the most revered of the poets he loved. The quotations he incorporates and presents as examples of the true muse are chiefly either lyrical, from Shelley, Keats, or pastoral poetry; or sublimely splendid, from Shakespeare or Milton or Dryden. He knows and reveres the classical world; he appears to have read widely in history, philosophy and anthropology, and to have pondered what he read. His heroes, who include Newton, Darwin, and Bertrand Russell, are those whose independent minds have kept reason alive, and those who, like Shelley and Shaw, have held out some earthly hope for humanity.

As to the manner of Purcell's assault, almost half *The Sweeniad* consists of either ironic or straightforward prose; the rest is in various styles of verse, many of which take the form of parody. The parodist's art is a delicate form of literary criticism, a criticism of style and sometimes also of the author's belief. It should not display the venom of satire, nor the boisterous humour of burlesque. Constant small surprises, quiet discrepancies, and pointed incongruities should alert the reader to the manner and thought of the author parodied. While expecting one thing, we encounter something slightly other. At his best, Purcell can do it skilfully. The parody of MacNeice 'It's no go the balanced life, it's no go St Xavier / All we want is a Cadillac, gin, and euthanasia' is neatly turned; as are the lines beginning 'Between the mystification / And the deception' which ape 'The Hollow Men'; and those needling 'Ash Wesnesday', 'I no longer want to want what you want me to want'. There are passages in 'The Vacant Mind' which precisely touch the nerve, and where the smiling art of the parodist is at its best:

> My uncle, he gave me a ride on a yak
> And I was speechless. He said, Mamie,
> Mamie, Mamie, grasp his ears . . .
> I drink most of the year and then I have a Vichy.

and:

> There I saw one I knew, and hailed him shouting,
>   Muravieff-Amursky!
> You who were with me up at Jesus,
> And fought in my battalion at Thermopylae!

The five lines beginning 'Your arms limp' are delicately done, as are those following 'Earthly limbo'; and, although the parodist's echoes wander a little in the middle of the Count Cagliostro section, they return happily enough for the last few lines.

The high-spirited confusion of the ending, with quotations from the liturgy, from Vachel Lindsay, Baudelaire, Lu Shih Ch'un Ch'iu (in Chinese), an Egyptian inscription (in Egyptian), the Morse Code, and deaf-and-dumb sign language, catches nicely the five languages and the piled quotations which end 'The Waste Land'. The 'Notes' to 'The Vacant Mind' vary from boisterous to witty, and some sharply point up the flavour of the originals ('"Life" here is an occult symbol for death'). The Notes proudly announce that 'The Vacant Mind' contains allusions and adaptations from thirty-five different writers in twenty languages, including Pali, Sanskrit, Aramaic, Tagalog, Swahili, and Bêche-de-mer.

Other passages elsewhere aptly echo Eliot's voice, including 'And yet I hear Lucretius in this cry / Of *rerum lacrimae*'; and certain of the Choruses ('Ah, what avails the sceptred race?' and 'The curse of spring') which, if not always precise parodies, deftly combine quotations and ideas from a wide variety of authors. In further parody of one of Eliot's favourite techniques, quotations abound throughout 'The Vacant Mind' from Schiller, Goethe, Shakespeare, Fitzgerald, Shelley, nursery rhyme, the Roman liturgy, and a host of other sources. Unfortunately there are also too many crudities of imagery and expression which break up the subtlety of the better sections:

> Pious sot!
> You have no guide or clue for you know only
> Puce snakes and violet mastodons . . .

and:

> I will show you fear in a pile of half-bricks

do little for the parodist's art.

The handling of the Postulator is vital to the irony of the whole. His task in presenting the case for Sweeney as 'poet, critic, sociologist, and man' is no sinecure, for Buttle can think of very little to say in Sweeney's favour. The Postulator's case is therefore undermined from the start, and his difficulties further emphasised by the preposterous views and practices he is obliged to support. Nevertheless, his view is presented with a consistent enthusiasm, behind which irony mischievously lurks. Solemnly he anatomises the profundities of 'The Vacant Mind', demonstrating how its confusion of elements exactly represents the confusion of modern life. Earnestly he explains how obscurity, absence of melody, and the pillaging of other men's work are all essential to true modernism. With eager approval he describes Sweeney's horror of social and domestic reform, and commends his belief in asceticism, and in the necessity of a dominating clerical hierarchy. Sometimes his stance wobbles; the ironic veil is rent, the anger of the author bursts through, and the argument becomes crudely sarcàstic or imbued with a venom too raw even for satire. But for much of his long task the Postulator keeps his end up well. His adversary, the Devil's Advocate, has the easier occupation in that he is squarely presenting the arguments of the author, without irony – and, sometimes, without much finesse.

The Sweeniad as a whole displays great vigour; the debate is well marshalled, and supplied with ample quotation from Sweeney's work. But clearly there are faults. The touch is sometimes deadly heavy, as in 'Paradise! Be importunate' and 'Orisons of the orgiastic Ebionite'; and in the dire parodies of the titles of Sweeney's poems. Other jarring effects sometimes spoil the flow; the arguments too often repeat themselves, and there are occasional passages[1] so irrelevant one can only suppose that the author, having composed them, could not bear to leave them out. The tone is sometimes crudely intemperate, defeating its own ends, and the humour can be schoolboyish ('Debag the blighter!'). The dream device, in which the entire work is cast, and the character of Myra herself, do not greatly convince.

To what extent has Purcell been just in his assessment of Eliot's attitudes and beliefs? No one would dispute that it was in the Christian message that Eliot sought salvation from the godless limbo of the modern world. In 1928 he publicly declared himself as an Anglo-Catholic, who saw in the doctrines of the Church the only possible redemption of man from the imperfect world he is born to.

---

[1] For instance, 'Cloax is the vilest drink' and 'In good King Edward's golden days' – the latter a breezy, skilful song.

Some of his views mellowed towards the end of his life, and he never permitted the reprinting of *After Strange Gods* (1934), in which he had expressed certain ideas in a form he later considered too emphatic. Nevertheless for many years he believed society to be 'worm-eaten with Liberalism' (1934), and detested the fashionable, feeble emphasis on tolerance and social reform. In his view this must give way to a positive Christian order, supervised by a priestly caste and a Christian elite – 'the only possible control and balance is a religious control and balance' (1939). Education must be controlled by the priestly hierarchy, for 'no adequate concept of education is possible without the leadership of the Church' (1965). Nor should it necessarily be available to all – 'A small number of people should be educated well, and others left with only a rudimentary education' (1948). To all this Purcell takes great exception, as any good humanist must. Eliot himself acknowledged the gulf between those for whom the doctrine of original sin is 'a very real and tremendous thing' and those for whom it is not (1934). And in an essay in *Revelation* (Baillie, 1937) he writes, 'The division between those who accept, and those who deny, Christian revelation I take to be the most profound difference between human beings.' In two essays on humanism (*Humanism*, 1928, and *Second Thoughts*, 1929) he attacks the humanist position with some vigour, and it does not appear that he later retracted his views. Clearly Purcell's insistence that some community of belief is essential to the appreciation of poetry is fundamental to his dislike of Eliot's work.

With some justice, Purcell considers Eliot's stance

as puritanical. F. O. Matthiessen, reflecting on the Puritan outlook, finds the problem of belief, a dry wit, a dread of vulgarity, a strong consciousness of evil, and a severe self-discipline among its chief characteristics (1935). It could hardly be denied that Eliot exhibits these signs, which represent a cast of mind entirely alien to Purcell. Yeats's description of Eliot's work as 'grey, cold, and dry' (1936) is echoed in Buttle's 'Who is he that cometh, like the flail of God / With a frigid stare, as cold as any cod'; and in the accusation that in Sweeney's work sex is invariably sterile, and all enjoyment of the physical self entirely absent.

In his criticism of Eliot's patronising attitude to the common man, Purcell could again be seen to have some justification. The few members of the working class who appear in Eliot's work are feebly realised, and his place for them in his Christian society does not seem enviable. In a withering comment, Harold Laski condemns Eliot's horror of the common man, and finds throughout his work 'a note of contempt and disdain for the masses' (1944). Nor, as Buttle indicates, is Eliot's attitude to Jews an attractive one; Bleistein, Klipstein and their fellows, together with the Jew spawned in the Antwerp *estaminet*, cannot be said to be presented with sympathy.

Eliot must now be allowed to defend himself against at least some of these charges. In writing over a span of nearly fifty years, he was likely to change his ideas from time to time, as any creative writer and thinker will. As he said in an essay on Yeats, 'A man who is capable of experience finds himself in a different world in every decade of his life' (1940). His poetic practice developed through several stages, and his views on, for instance, Milton, Yeats, and the relative merits of Shakespeare and Dante also changed noticeably over the years. Yet he was constantly accused of holding ideas he had modified or abandoned perhaps long before, and in his last collection of essays he protested at this practice (1965). Nevertheless many of his beliefs and attitudes did not alter greatly, and he confronts at some point most of the problems and objections raised by Buttle. F. O. Matthiessen (1935) quotes a lecture of Eliot's at Yale in 1933, which vividly points the gulf between his own view of poetry and that of Purcell: '. . . to write poetry with nothing poetic about it, poetry standing naked in its bare bones . . . or poetry so transparent that . . . we are intent on what the poem *points at*, and not on the poetry, that seems to me the thing to try for.' He argues that the 'meaning' of the poem may keep the reader soothed while the poem does its work, or indeed that the poet may seek intensity through the deliberate elimination of meaning (1933). Again, the meaning may be more than the poet knows, and if the poem is hard to paraphrase this may be because 'the poet is occupied with frontiers of consciousness beyond which words fail' (*Music*, 1942). The poem may be obscure because the experience cannot be expressed directly, or because the subject or the method are new, or because the reader expects difficulty, or because the expected has been omitted (1933). As with the metaphysical poets, who wrote before, in Eliot's words, the 'dissociation of sensibility' set in, so a modern poet writing in a disintegrated society must be 'more complex, more allusive, more indirect, in order to force, to dislocate if necessary, language into his meaning' (*Metaphysical*, 1921). In defence of elites, so much disliked by Purcell, Eliot argues that in a time of social disruption the artist is cut off from the larger public and can expect only a small, exclusive audience (*Classics*, 1942).

As to the nature of poetic language, Eliot points out that 'A great many second-rate poets . . . have not the sensitivity and consciousness to preceive that they feel differently from the preceding generation, and therefore must use words differently' (*London*, 1930). Again and again[1] he returns to the subject of a poet's language; indeed with such emphasis that Wyndham Lewis noted with satisfaction that Eliot had instilled in his young followers 'a salutary *fear of speech – a terror of the word*' (1934). In the Introduction to Marianne Moore Eliot declares that 'the poet is carrying on that struggle for the maintenance of a living language . . . which must be kept up in every generation'. For the poet's language must be that of recognisable speech; if it has in the course of time become too elaborate, and lost touch with the common idiom, it must be recalled to its daily form (*Music*, 1942). This is another point at which Purcell parts company with Eliot. His own view, implied in *Cadmus*, is that a poetic language should decidedly not be the language of everyday speech.

Concerning the 'beauties' of poetry, which Purcell finds much neglected in Eliot's work, Eliot holds

---

[1] Perhaps most fruitfully in his Introduction to the *Selected Poems of Marianne Moore* (1935) and in 'The Music of Poetry' (1942).

that most words on their own are neither beautiful nor ugly; those which are rich must not be allowed to overload the whole, and obtrusive imagery must be avoided. The music of verse, like the music of notes – to which his work constantly aspires – should not be apparent line by line, but should be a music of the whole (*Music*, 1942). Words should perform as they are described in 'Little Gidding', as a 'complete consort, dancing together'. And as to the vocabulary of poetry, he believed it should be sought deeper than the heart – in the brain, the nervous system, the digestion, and any place in which sustenance might be found, including the horrors of the twentieth-century metropolis (*Metaphysical*, 1921). He describes how he himself learned from Baudelaire 'a precedent for the poetical possibilities . . . of the more sordid aspects of the modern metropolis, of the possibility of fusion between the sordidly realistic and the phantasmagoric' (1950). It is clear that Purcell strongly objected to such sources of poetic vocabulary.

He also deplores the lack of metrical structure and rhyme, and the general chaotic freedom of modern verse. But Eliot makes clear his conviction that good 'free' verse can never be free, for it must retain at least the ghost of a simple metre (*Reflections*, 1917). Metrical forms and conventions may sometimes need to be broken, not in the perverse hope of liberation but because a contemporary living form must be constantly sought and found (*Music*, 1942). As to the rejection of rhyme, he believes that far from making the poet's task easier rejection makes it harder, because words become more exposed (*Reflections*, 1917).

Often in his prose writings Eliot returns to the relationship of the poet to his poem. While he has no doubt that 'what every poet starts from is his own emotions' (*Shakespeare*, 1927) he is equally clear that the next task is to perform 'a continual extinction of the personality' in such a way that the poet who suffers and the poet who creates become almost separate beings (*Tradition*, 1919). And indeed he always detested the aggrandisement of personality, and never gave his highest praise to the kind of personal poetry known as 'Romantic'. As Purcell's reverence is chiefly reserved for poets of direct and intense feeling, this impersonality of Eliot's work is not pleasing to him. Nor does he have any time for Eliot's 'objective correlative', by means of which images are transformed into an impersonal formula which carries the poet's emotion.

Allied to his liking for a direct effusion of feeling, and to his admiration for quotable phrases, is Purcell's belief that 'beauty' and 'greatness' are qualities to which the critic's finger can readily point. With this view Eliot strongly disagrees. There are, he believes, no criteria of sublimity or greatness, art never 'improves', and as each generation is interested in art in its own way there can be no abiding standards of appreciation (*Tradition*, 1919). If poetry is to live, new traditions and new forms of appreciation must be allowed to grow, and the mark of a good critic will be the ability to select a good new poem by responding to a new situation (1933).

Purcell is again at odds with Eliot in the matter of tradition. He feels that modern poetry has broken away from the past, and that the aim of the moderns, led by Sweeney, was to cut themselves off from these nourishing roots and attempt the hopeless task of beginning again. Nothing could be further from Eliot's thought. Time and again he emphasises the vital function of a tradition growing from the past and adapting itself to the present. Tradition is not, in his belief, fossilised and hostile to change; new traditions must arise, and sentimentality about the past must not be allowed to stifle them. New poetry, he maintained, has significance only in relation to the poetry of the past, and each new poet in some way modifies the past order (*Tradition*, 1919). He notes that in his Cantos Pound achieves 'a final concentration of the entire past upon the present' (*Method*, 1919), and in his own poetry his hope was to do the same.

As for 'The Waste Land', Eliot himself made some highly derogatory comments – though it is not easy to decide how seriously he meant them to be taken. His brother Henry records him as having said, 'To me it was only the relief of a personal and wholly insignificant grouse against life; it is just a piece of rhythmical grumbling.'[1] Again, when asked in an interview recorded in the *Paris Review* (1963) whether Pound had changed the intellectual structure of the poem, he replied, 'No, I think it was just as structureless, only in a more futile way, in the longer version.' He further commented, 'I wasn't even bothering whether I understood what I was saying.' And elsewhere he refers to his Notes to the poem as 'a remarkable exposition of bogus scholarship' (1965). It was unfortunate for Purcell that he

---

[1] Quoted at the beginning of the facsimile edition of 1971.

evidently never saw these comments – how avidly he would have pounced.

As we have seen, Buttle objected to Sweeney's effrontery in presuming to take on the mantle of Johnson and Arnold. Certainly Eliot took something of this weight upon himself, but the degree of his effrontery must be left for the reader to decide. F. R. Leavis considered him a critic capable of 'a mastery of genius' (1969), and F. O. Matthiessen saw in *The Sacred Wood* no less than a critical revolution (1935). Whatever his critical practice, Eliot's objectives are unexceptionable. A good critic, he declared, applies himself to the double task of deciding what is poetry and what is a good poem (1933); and sees as 'the great, the perennial task of criticism the miracle of bringing the poet back to life' (*Marvell*, 1921). To these aims Purcell does not object. He does, however, take strong exception to the moral and religious attitudes he detects behind much of the criticism. Eliot came to believe firmly in the necessity of a moral view, and unequivocally asserted that 'literary criticism should be completed by criticism from a definite ethical and theological standpoint' (*Religion*, 1935); and that the critic and the reader should know both what they like and what they *ought* to like. Purcell feels this moral stance to be beyond the proper bounds of criticism. Nor does he care for Eliot's magisterial delivery. He should perhaps have given him some credit for a high degree of self-awareness in this matter, for Eliot well knew how formidable he could be. In the Preface to the second edition of *The Sacred Wood* he disarmingly apologises for previous 'pontifical solemnity'; later he repudiates his reputation for learning (*Classics*, 1942); and at the end of his career again apologises for various errors, including those of 'tone' (1965).

It will by now be apparent that, in spite of the fact that both men, in their different ways, loved poetry and cared about the moral and social welfare of their fellows, Eliot and Purcell did not share much in the way of temperament or attitude. Indeed, a chasm yawns. The religious themes to which Eliot devoted much of his working life were anathema to Purcell. Constantly he makes plain his dislike of Christian thought – yet he devotes surprisingly little time to the *Four Quartets*, briefly dismissing them as 'a mere vehicle for conveying the formal doctrines of the Church'. The plays too receive rather less than the minimum of attention.

On the problem of 'meaning', Eliot agrees (1933) with the pronouncement of I. A. Richards that 'it is never what a poem *says* that matters, but what it *is*' (1924). He believed that the enjoyment of a poem is not dependent on understanding, nor on the sharing of the poet's belief, but is likely to be richer if belief is shared (1929). This view he slightly modified when he added that if the poet's belief was worthy of respect it would not hinder the enjoyment of the non-believing reader (1933). This belief that the overt content of a poem was not important was hotly contested by Purcell, in company with many other critics. In trying to avoid this difficulty, Spender wisely directs attention away from the rigidity of Eliot's doctrinal theory in order to emphasise the powerful sense of mystery and the visionary aspects of his belief (1975); but Purcell would probably not have found this interpretation convincing or helpful.

On this wide but honest opposition of view little need be said, except that it seems to have precluded the kind of sympathetic attention a critic should grant his subject. Blinkered by his rationalist beliefs, Purcell was unwilling to look for what there might be in heaven and earth beyond them. For it must be admitted that there is much in Eliot's work that he did not make any great effort to understand. Confined in his foursquare approach, he could not surrender himself to the total effect of a poem; and because of the opposition of his beliefs could not react sympathetically to Eliot's Christian philosophy. Even before Eliot's concerns became specifically Christian, he finds the social and ethical attitudes distasteful.

But perhaps the most serious of his shortcomings as a critic of Eliot is his resistance to the mythic and symbolic aspects of the poetry. Eliot had an abiding interest in the primitive functioning of the creative mind. Beginning to write at a time when 'Imagist' and 'Symbolist' were new and exciting words, he was intensely aware of the power of the symbol, which he described in the *Dial* as 'an image of the making conscious, an image which combines the precise and concrete with a kind of almost infinite suggestion' (1928). Several critics[1] have explored this vital process of the 'making conscious', and emphasised the importance of Eliot's symbols in transmuting his personal emotion into experience of

---

[1] Most recently A. D. Moody (1979) and Grover Smith (1983).

general significance. Robert Langbaum indicates how Eliot's use of symbols in 'The Waste Land' sets up echoing parallels between the overt and the buried, especially in the ancient rituals of chess, cards, and cleansing with water (Litz, 1973); clearly a reader to whom these kinds of images are dead will not find satisfaction in Eliot's work.

Moving on to the problem of obscurity, Johan Fabricius shows how through the use of universal, unconscious symbols the twentieth-century artist transmutes the experience of his civilisation into 'a psychological mood or inner vision', and in so doing inevitably creates difficult work which is likely to be accused of obscurity (1958). On a similar theme, Herbert Read traces the great changes in art and science throughout this century, and shows how they have led to changes in modes of perception. The artist has been compelled to find new symbols to represent new states of mind, and in so doing has found himself on new frontiers, giving shape to uncertain intuitions. He will of course suffer abuse, and the condemnation of those who fear corrupters of the old traditions (1955).

In an essay particularly relevant to *The Sweeniad*, Philip Wheelwright considers the fallacy of 'semantic atomism' – an inelegant but useful phrase to describe the assumption that open, straightforward statements are quite sufficient for all purposes of communication (Rajan, 1947). Like many who see themselves as plain, honest dealers, Purcell is inclined to cherish the fallacy of semantic atomism; Myra, in her Preface, speaks with some pride of her own plain, unvarnished words. But, because of the difficulty of what he has to say, Eliot must be often difficult. Cleanth Brooks shows how Eliot deliberately applied 'the principle of complexity' in his use of omission, contrast, irony and other devices (Rajan, 1947); these, Eliot evidently felt, were essential complexities in pursuing the 'logic of the imagination', which he held to be as valid as the 'logic of concepts' (Perse, 1930). F. R. Leavis returns often to Eliot's skill in giving compressed definition to fleeting perception (1932, 1969); and Helen Gardner points to his willingness to demand patience of the reader while he advances and retreats, awaiting the moment described by Keats when 'several things dovetailed' in his mind (Rajan, 1947). Eliot himself describes how in the poet's mind 'impressions and experiences combine in peculiar and unexpected ways', which may, because of their novelty, be difficult for the reader to understand (*Tradition*, 1919).

As we have seen, Purcell felt that modern poetry had made a disastrous break with tradition. But many critics have pointed out that in spite of his originality Eliot's work is steeped in tradition, and that he searched constantly for traditional principles which could be related to contemporary life. His use of allusion and quotation, so roundly condemned by Purcell, is clearly related to his belief in the perpetual presence of the past, and fundamental to his technique. Purcell cannot come to terms with it, regarding it as no better than thieving. Clearly he was stoutly opposed to all those critics who have shown how these allusions perform a function of concentration, creating what Grover Smith happily describes as 'a music of allusions' (1983). Indeed I. A. Richards, writing of 'The Waste Land', believed that the quotations performed such a work of concentration that without them the poem would have to be of epic length (1924). The language so freely borrowed from the liturgy performs the same concentrating, impersonal function. The technique of quotation contributes also to the kind of compression described by Geoffrey Bullough, whereby Eliot attempts 'to see the theme from several angles in the shortest possible time', as if he were translating into words the many-faceted paintings of Picasso (1962).

Whatever the rights and wrongs of his antagonism, Purcell did not stand alone. We have seen that his attack on Eliot's poetry is centred almost entirely on 'The Waste Land'. This difficult work still provokes much argument, not all of it alien to Purcell's point of view. In *The Sweeniad* the Devil's Advocate concedes that 'The Vacant Mind' is a landmark in English poetry, and that for good or ill it became enormously influential. Moreover the workmanship of the early work revealed him as a master craftsman, and the breadth of his scholarship cannot be denied. But, given these meagre concessions, there is little else Purcell is prepared to grant. For instance, he objects strongly that beyond a reference to a demobbed soldier Eliot does not mention in 'The Waste Land' the appalling experience of the First World War. And there were others who found 'The Waste Land' less than universal in its theme. Spender saw it as representing the post-war experience of an isolated sensibility, in a small class of intellectuals (1935); E. M. Forster thought it 'just a personal comment on the universe' (1936); and Eliot himself insisted that it did not express 'the disillusion of a generation' (1931).

In deploring the deathly pessimism of the poem, Purcell is again not alone. Its message of hopelessness has been emphasised by many, and indeed those who find some hint of hope are few and far between. As to the manner and structure of the poem, Purcell does not seriously seek to fathom it. It is, to paraphrase his Advocate, a disastrous collision of the Old Morality and the Old Tradition with the new heresy of Science and Modern Learning, filled out with scraps from jazz, the gutter press, and irrelevant quotation. Many critics would agree. Much of great interest has been written on the unity (or otherwise) of 'The Waste Land', from Leavis's famous passage beginning 'The unity the poem aims at is that of an inclusive consciousness' (1932) to the many objections of those who see an insoluble problem in the poem's lack of structure. The work of Joseph Frank on the 'spatial' as opposed to the 'temporal' dimensions of modern poetry (1945) links usefully with Eliot's essay on Pound, much of which might well be an observation on his own work in 'The Waste Land': 'the casual or lazy reader will find . . . only a succession of bright discrete images, and a collection of obscure literary allusions. . . . The more discerning will find careful study of the compression of the essential points of a story or situation' (1917). Hugh Kenner's view that Pound's excisions from the original 'Waste Land' left 'the luminous bits to discover their own unexpected affinities' (Litz, 1973) echoes something of Eliot's words on Pound.

Was Purcell the kind of 'casual or lazy reader'

referred to by Eliot? Whatever the answer, he had many companions whose censures were not unlike his own. It is now time to consider the more aggressive voices among the anti-Eliot critics, to whose protests Buttle added her indignant cry. How far does Purcell articulate the sentiments of the large and growing band who express, at the one pole, thoughtful reservations, and at the other vitriolic denunciations of Eliot's work? So solidly has his reputation become established it is not always easy to remember how entrenched an opposition flourishes and grows. In general terms, the long uproar over 'The Waste Land' was succeeded, about 1930, by a period of acceptance and calm, when Eliot's enormous reputation was not seriously or publicly challenged – however many grumblings remained below the surface. A new dissaffection seems to have set in some time in the late thirties, and to have increased in volume over the last twenty-five years or so.

Prufrock and other Observations appeared in 1917 and was not widely noticed, although Arthur Waugh, reviewing it in the *Quarterly Review*, described its author as 'a drunken helot' – a view to which not many took exception. 'The Waste Land' first appeared in this country in the October number of the *Criterion*, 1922, and in the *Dial* in New York in November; but it did not arouse much interest in England until the publication of the Hogarth Press edition in 1923. Immediately opinion was violently divided. Many supposed the poem was a hoax, and Eliot had publicly to deny the rumour; many others thought it was not meant to be a poem at all, but a slightly related series of separate poems. *The Times*

Literary Supplement questioned its power to move, and found it parodying 'without taste or skill'; although there was a scattering of pearls among the litter, it regretted the sordidity of the urban images, and found Eliot to be 'walking very near the limits of coherence' (20 September 1923). F. L. Lucas in the *New Stateman*, roundly supporting J. C. Squire in the *London Mercury*, scorned 'the catchwords of renunciation' and the fertility-ritual, but in looking for quotable lines (reminiscent of Purcell's later practice) found at the beginning 'one of the snatches of poetry that occur scattered about the poem'. Arnold Bennett, Edmund Gosse, and A. E. Housman were among other eminent men of letters who joined in the general condemnation. In the United States Louis Untermeyer described the poem as 'a piece of literary carpentry, scholarly joiner's work . . . a pompous parade of erudition' (1923).

Conrad Aiken, Edmund Wilson and a few others were writing very much more sympathetically, though not always with total enthusiasm. In the *Dial* Wilson defended Eliot by emphasising the creative strength and vigour of his poetry. He admired in 'The Waste Land' 'the hunger for beauty and the anguish at living' but he could not admire the apparent lack of structure (1922). Aiken, a staunch friend and defender, writing in the *New Republic*, praised the emotional coherence of the work, finding that its parts created an ensemble, like a tone poem in music, but he too could not find any rational unity. He thought the work seemed like a series of separate poems; the mythical material was not properly assimilated; and Eliot's use of quotation was merely parasitic (1923).

It is interesting to see how these early objections, none later than 1923, foreshadow so much of the antagonistic criticism that was yet to come. Eliot's inability to create a solid logical structure; his pessimism; his ostentatious learning; the sordidity of his imagery, and his inability to write quotable lines; his insistence on the importance of renunciation; his inability to absorb mythic material; and his extensive use of allusion and quotation – all these objections may be found in the early years, and all were to be frequently echoed from that time to the present.

When Edmund Wilson enlarged the scope of his earlier work on 'The Waste Land' he opened up another theme which has constantly recurred, and which was an important element in Purcell's dislike. Wilson finds 'an ascetic shrinking from sexual experience', symbolised in the impotence of the Fisher King, and, he supposes, indirectly a result of Eliot's puritan background (1931). A few years later Hugh Ross Williamson proposed sex as the central problem of the poem, whose message points as a solution to the saving virtues of asceticism and the love of God (1932). These suggestions have been widely taken up and amplified by all those who, like Purcell, regard Eliot's work as devitalised and essentially against life.

By about 1930 Eliot's position in the literary world was established to a degree which incensed his detractors, who began to multiply. One whose severe work must be taken seriously is Yvor Winters, who maintained a long and impenitent attack on all aspects of Eliot's work. He finds almost nothing commendable, either poetic or critical, but he marshals his arguments to good effect, and he knows Eliot's work. He is concerned at the extent to which, he asserts, Eliot contradicts himself, not only in his critical judgement but in the theory and practice of his own work. Although Eliot abhors determinism, his thought, in Winters's view, tends strongly towards a deterministic view of literature. He defines and analyses 'the fallacy of imitative form', to which, he believed, too many critics had resorted in an attempt to justify the lack of structure in Eliot's work. Chaos and disintegration cannot be conveyed by simply imitating them. In debating the question of meaning and obscurity he cannot agree with Eliot that the material enforced upon the poet, as the vehicle of his emotion, is of no importance. The feeling expressed in a work of art, Winters believes, must originate in the artist's understanding of his subject. If, as Eliot asserts, the emotion arises first, and the intellectual content is not of the first importance, then the writer can produce only 'a formless reverie'. He finds the influence of Eliot wholly dangerous, and believes it has achieved 'the benumbing energy of a bad habit', and that critics who protest are dismissed as not of the elect. It will be noticed how many of these views are shared by Purcell.

The next full-blooded assault came from R. H. Robbins (1951). Vehemently he deplores the reputation and influence of Eliot, as both poet and critic. Many readers, he declares, admit to not understanding him, others tamely disregard what meaning they do happen to understand, and most people cannot read him at all; yet no adverse voice is raised and the writings continue to be worshipped.[1]

---

[1] Eliot-worship arose in the 1920s, and was attacked as early as 1930 by Sherry Mangan in *A Note: on the somewhat Premature Apotheosis of T. S. Eliot*.

Embarking on one of the perennial debates, Robbins asserts that Eliot and his followers, in holding that the overt meaning of a poem is not important to appreciation, are responsible for the disastrous divorce in poetry of content and form. He points with aversion to Eliot's dislike of his fellow men, to the sterility of sex in his work, and to the antisemitism. He deplores the insistence on a religiously based education, and the despair which sees life as merely a preparation for death. He believes, with Purcell, that after Eliot's conversion in 1928 his work can mean little to those who do not share his faith; and that his increasingly heavy use of a religious vocabulary must alienate most of his readers. The best poetry, he considers, is found in the early work, where it is unhampered by theology; by the time of the publication of 'Ash Wednesday' in 1930 the sermonising was blatant, and the *Four Quartets* are no more than a 'versified tractate'. Eliot's political and social attitudes involved an admiration for 'clerico-fascism', a contempt for democracy, and disdain for all those less well educated than himself. It is surely clear that Purcell had read this book and found in it, among much else, the first full exposition of the 'conspiracy' theory, which held that Eliot's reputation was based not on his own excellence but on the support of the 'Establishment' and the political right, who regarded him with gratitude and saw to it that he was piled with honours, including the OM and the Nobel Prize. Robbins concedes that Eliot had some metrical skill, and a fine 'mobility' in his prose, but concludes that he was 'a poet of minor achievement, emotionally sterile and with a mind coarsened by snobbery and constrained by bigotry'.

David Daiches makes plain his high admiration for Eliot, but expresses reservations, not unlike Purcell's, on the poet's lack of 'sympathetic imagination' and of simple human compassion (1958). Two further thoughtful but determined assaults were made in 1960, one by Graham Hough and one by David Craig. Hough, writing on 'The Waste Land', insists that whatever attempts have been made to find some unifying principle the poem is ultimately chaotic; and that in spite of Eliot's 'Note' Tiresias does nothing to increase its coherence. He challenges Eliot's belief that there is a logic of the imagination as well as a logic of concepts, and insists that a poem must make the same kind of sense as any other form of words; a mere collection of images, however striking, cannot be sufficient in themselves. Eliot's theory that 'meaning' may be offered as a distraction while the poem does its real work cannot be justified. He objects strongly to the technique of allusion and quotation ('a barbarous, tasteless hewing up of gobbets'), and on various counts finds Eliot's communication with his reader faulty. But he adds that, happily, Eliot's practice frequently belies his principles.

David Craig takes up the much-debated subject of Eliot's denial of life; he himself sees 'The Waste Land' as basically pessimistic, and working essentially against hope. In 1972 and again in 1977 F. W. Bateson published important work on Eliot's deficiencies. Among various other observations, he accuses Eliot of an appearance of erudition which is not backed with true scholarship. For his own stimulus rather than for his poetry, Eliot needed the excitement of learning, or at least of 'a masquerade of scholarship'. Although he considers Eliot the best critic since Arnold, he detects confusion in the theory of 'the dissociation of sensibility', and finds the early critical work to be strewn with errors. He sees the poet as having a magpie's eye for bright fragments, dislikes the number of plagiarisms he detects, and finds that in the later work the allusions and quotations become merely a mannerism, eking out thin material. 'The Waste Land' he sees as chaotic and pretentious, and in his final judgement considers Eliot to be only a good minor poet, but for all his faults a major literary critic.

Several contributors to Graham Martin's symposium (1970) take up positions hostile to Eliot; Terry Eagleton, by implication rather than statement, deprecates his emphasis on the need for a hierarchical Christian society, and Ian Hamilton, writing on 'The Waste Land', attacks the display of cultural wealth in the excessive use of quotation, flattering those who know 'the cultural score'. Like Hough, he finds no unifying personality at the centre of the poem, dislikes the hints of sexual revulsion, and finds a revealing contrast between Eliot's own crippling refinement and the crippling vulgarity of most of mankind.

In 1972 the young poet James Simmons published a narrative stanzaic poem, or series of poems, relating the story of his Irish country childhood, his poverty in London, his attempts to become a writer, and his eventual achievement of a Gregory Award, given him by a committee which ironically included T. S. Eliot. What unifies his poems, he declares, is their reaction against the fashionable anti-life attitude, most famously exemplified in 'The Waste Land'. And indeed his poem echoes with allusions to Eliot's work. The character named 'Stearns' is intended 'to stand for the uptight quality in all of us', and the main thrust of the argument – more memorable than the narrative – is against the work of Eliot, who 'continues to make ordinary people seem disgusting'. Eliot's Londoners, says Simmons, are 'just as phoney as Yeats's Irish peasants'. He cries of Stearns's waste land of London, 'Where does this lurid vision touch reality?' Defecation, copulation, vomit and smoke, which Stearns finds so repellent, Simmons sees as healthy evidence that people are alive and not dead. In this plain man's guide to living, Simmons declares 'I never found Spring cruel', and with heavy irony calls on Stearns to 'come round to meet the boys tonight / To see the hollow men get full and tight'. There is no evidence that Simmons had read *The Sweeniad*, but, in his dislike of elitism, pessimism, and the sterile forces which oppose the full life, he shares much with Purcell.

Donald Davie's work has been on the whole admiring of Eliot, but he finds a touch of the parochial, home-counties atmosphere in Eliot's attitudes, reminiscent of Purcell's 'gloomy maze set up in the Vicarage garden'; and finds too that as a social critic Eliot undermines his own thinking by dreaming of a medieval peasantry and refusing to recognise the existence of a vast and irremovable proletariat (Litz, 1973).

The most recent of the whole-hearted assaults on Eliot and his reputation was by Kenneth Hopkins (1976). Taking a chronological track through Eliot's work, he finds nothing to praise, even in the early poems. The originality of *Prufrock* (1917) was, he believes, merely superficial, as the manner and techniques had already been explored by G. M. Hopkins, Whitman, Pound, and the Sitwells. Eliot's work is in fact almost all derivative, and has never added anything valuable to the English poetic tradition. *Poems 1920* exhibits the arrogance, obscurity, triviality, and parade of useless learning of a second-class mind – strictures we have begun to recognise. 'The Waste Land', a bogus and ephemeral work, significant to only a small band of contemporaries, confirms the impression of poetic inadequacy. 'The Hollow Men' is the best of the early 'pieces of pompous froth'; but with the publication of 'Ash Wednesday' ('the balance-sheet of a chief executive') Eliot is pretentiously established in the nation's Chair of Poetry and Criticism. The *Four Quartets* he grants to be the best of the poetry, but believes that they have achieved a grossly exaggerated importance through the publicity accorded them. Their influence is only negative and sterile. As to the criticism, Eliot is not a lover of poetry, but 'a giver of laws', who kills whatever he anatomises, and whose statements are received by critics and public 'as though they emanated from the Vatican'. Hopkins blames the critics as much as the author, because they have allowed themselves to be led sheepishly astray until there is no honest, uncomplimentary criticism of Eliot to be heard. As a critic, Hopkins concludes, Eliot has done great harm, and as a poet his reputation has been inflated far beyond that suitable for the minor poet that he was.

Enough has now been said to show that Myra Buttle's angry cry was far from solitary, and that she voiced many of the criticisms which constantly recur in the writings of those who dislike Eliot's work. Many of these criticisms have their sources in deep divisions of temperament and belief as much as in critical judgement; and, if this is so, are likely to flourish as long as Eliot's work is read. It looks as if there will always be rebellious voices protesting against the adulation that has come Sweeney's way.

MYRA BUTTLE
THE SWEENIAD

PREFACE

I AM only a very ordinary girl, and what with my grandmother being bedridden and my having to give a hand in the shop, I am kept pretty busy. But I do find time to read, and poetry is about as necessary to me as air, though, of course, I don't need it quite so often or in such quantities. However, the more I read of modern poetry since Yeats, the more exasperated did I become—not so much with its obscurity as with its argument. I am speaking, mind you, of the so-called "Main Stream", whose course was diverted in 1922 to join the Styx, not of the poetry of a few sturdy independents, such as Robert Graves or William Empson. The underlying message of the "Main Stream" poets seems to be that life is a sorry business anyhow, but that it might just be worth losing if, as an interim measure, we could undo the Renaissance and restore the Middle Ages, thereby making everybody as miserable as ourselves. Being a healthy girl with a good appetite, engaged to be married to a judo champion, this was too much for me to swallow and I was kept awake at night worrying about it all.

Then one night I had a dream. Like most dreams it was a bit of a jumble, but it seemed to be about modern poetry starting off on the wrong foot, then struggling a little towards the daylight, but finally getting bogged down. When I woke up I wrote it all out in my plain consumer's words, adding a few comments of my own. In the hope that it may interest others, I am having it printed and am presenting copies to a few carefully selected individuals. Any reaction from them, whether sympathetic or otherwise, would be much appreciated.

MYRA BUTTLE

I
THE GHOST THEATRE

NARRATOR
>The orchestra has packed up. The singers who entertained us so divinely have left for Elysium by helicopter, train, or inter-galactic rocket.
>Most of the audience is dead, for (as Wordsworth says) "The good die first, and they whose hearts are dry as summer dust burn to the socket."
>Good night, Mr Shakespeare, I am sorry you must go and have to travel so far,
>I will look for you out of my telescope as you pass by the morning star.
>It has been a memorable evening. The soloists were accompanied on lute, virginals, spinet, harpsichord, or pianoforté,
>Except for John Donne who insisted on having a theorbo, being characteristically perverse and haughty.
>As we listened, we lived through century after century and passed from continent to continent in the birth, flowering, and maturity of the English and (in a minor way) the American soul.
>Reverberating in our ears are echoes—"the cloud-capp'd towers, the gorgeous palaces", "multitudinous seas incarnadine", "O, Wild West Wind, thou breath of Autumn's being", "perilous seas in faery lands forlorn", "like those Nicèan barks of yore"—all well-worn clichés, no doubt, and diverse and fragmentary, but combining into a magnificent whole.

For a while we sit in silence, rehearsing the performance all over again in our minds, but the fact is that one cannot live indefinitely on memory alone,
Or be satisfied by the replacement of the rich voicings of the basses, baritones, tenors, and an occasional soprano by "unheard melodies" or "ditties of no tone".
While we are fidgeting and drumming our fingers on the sides of the seats someone begins to hum,
But, irritating as it is, for a long time no one has the heart to silence the silly bum.
Then partly to drown the noise and partly to while away the time,
Some of us extemporize songs on the traditional model with all the paraphernalia of caesura, enjambment, classical allusion, and interlocking rhyme.
But the effect is self-conscious and jejune,
Like a worn-out phonographic tune,
Altogether out of keeping with the sounds that come through to us from the streets outside the concert-hall.
In fact, it won't do at all.
The disjointed rhythms of contemporary life, the lack of stability, the screeching of brakes, sudden death, and the muffled roar of the traffic
Simply won't accept the discipline of blank verse, sonnet, stichomyth, hexameter, or sapphic,
Any more than "Of Man's first disobedience and the fruit of that forbidden tree"
Will fit into a boogiewoogie melody.
The only metres that seem to function nowadays are electric, water, gasoline, or taxi,
(Though it may be quite different for all I know on the northern shores of the Caspian or the Black Sea).

CHORUS
This vast unlighted room
Is the symbol of the tomb
And likewise of the womb.

Then someone has an inspiration (I think his name is
   Bolonsky, or Stubbs, or it may even be Antrobus);
Climbing up on to the empty platform he solemnly
   addresses us thus:

"For better or for worse,
Ours is no longer the one and only universe,
And Dryden's 'From harmony, from heavenly
   harmony, the universal frame began'
Is bunk. Likewise his 'diapason closing full in Man'.
What's more, this flattened beehive called the Milky
   Way
(Five thousand light-years thick, the pundits say)
Is, for all its vast immeasurable mass,
Only a few trivial molecules of gas;
Our sun, which used to 'flatter the mountain tops with
   sovereign eye',
Is just a living lie,
A tiny point of light,
One of the meanest of the 'meaner beauties of the
   night';
As for 'this goodly frame, the earth',
Why, it's no more than a microbe's testicle in girth,
And far from being the unique stronghold of the
   Master Race, is, so far as speculation probes,
Only one of many millions of inhabitable globes.

"As with the Macro- so with the Microcosm,
A granite mountain, a maggot, or a lady's bosom
(Pardon me this parity)

Are nothing but a mass of wildly moving particles
   rushing round and round without any apparent
   law or regularity
(Though it turns out that the nucleus and electrons,
   those denizens of the thinnest air,
Like the sun and planets, do at least obey the mathe-
   matical law of inverse-square).
Truth (it sounds like Jesting Pilate turned sophistical)
Is only relative and statistical.
And, in conclusion, let me make this clear,
Those passions that you hold most dear
Are only complexes and neuroses,
Lesions and psychoses,
What you call 'love' is really your *libido*,
Whether you be Dante or Petrarch, or only Little Dog
   Fido,
And this holds true from Poughkeepsie to Hokkaido.
Here is the theme, the romance, the pabulum
   humdinger
For the Twentieth-Century singer.
To work, ye unborn bards, fear not to make
   cacophony,
For Science has no ear and will not let you off any."

The instant that Hodges (or was it Mantalini?) uttered
   this manifesto,
The Traditional Ovum raped by the Marxian Sperm
Became a squirming germ,
   Hey Presto!

CHORUS
Myriads of minute metronomes
Baton the Ballet of the Chromosomes;
The solo-dancing of unmated genes
Conjures up visions of the might-have-beens.

A VOICE
>   *Paradise! Be importunate, the living heart,*
>   *Hemmed in by shipwreck, occultly inarticulate,*
>   *Conceives the total knighthood and twists the ribbon,*
>   *Tutorizing the proscenium of the equinoctial tract.*
>   *But the certainty of pneumatic equity,*
>   *Lit by the eyes of stoats, coldly at the rehearsal,*
>   *Contrives euphoric syntax like a neural itch,*
>   *Ecstatic triumph for the padded prothesis,*
>   *Bringing the embedded beeswax into dim perusal.*

NARRATOR
Who's that up in the gallery? What's he trying to convey?
The Second Law of Thermodynamics, did you say?
"When the position and velocity of molecules are distributed absolutely at random the entropy is complete."
Bravo, my boy! Your obfuscation is a treat,
The words are in the dictionary; the syntax is correct—
Reductio ad absurdum of the "Indirect"!
But though your talent cannot be denied,
Some may think you would be better occupied
Sitting in the kitchen doing your philately,
Or in the WC, re-writing *Lady Chatterley*.

Thermodynamics?
These molecules must be like Victor Hugo's *djinns*—
What a universe away from Keats's eternity-ceramics!

CHORUS
>   It will not change, though it will grow
>   This neo-Georgian verse in embryo.

A VOICE

>*It's no go your Church and State, it's no go Tradition,*
>*All we want is a heck of a time, in and out of prison.*
>*Yell for the Dodgers on TV, till they fuse to curry.*
>*Shove his face in the cuspidor—the cop's your only buddy.*
>
>*Lorelei, she wed a guy, met him back in Reno,*
>*Shot him three times in the eye as he played the piano.*
>*Pregnant by her husbands four, no jury would convict her.*
>*Now she's wed her alienist;* News-Post *has their picture.*
>
>*It's no go the Balanced Life; it's no go St Xavier,*
>*All we want is a Cadillac, gin, and euthanasia.*

NARRATOR

>Ah, a people's poet from the body of the hall!
>At least the *meaning* of his little ballad's clear to all.
>His *oedipus* was knocked around when he was small.
>(Note. This allegory replaces that of Adam and the Fall).
>As for Lorelei, poor kid,
>Her *ego* got entangled with her *id*,
>Much as her ancestor's in Eden did,
>Not to mention the *imago*
>Of her mómma from Oswego.
>And yet I hear Lucretius in this cry
>Of *rerum lacrimae.*
>One thing more —
>The rhyming is by Heisenberg and Bohr.
>
>Hello! Here comes another voice from what should be the "Stalls"

(It's hard to say precisely where in a building with no
   walls).
Another thing I find so odd about this ghostly place is
That though it's full of people, you cannot see their
   faces,
And when you hear a voice and try to fix its owner
   with a glance,
He simply moves aside as if avoiding your advance,
And all the feeble light reveals is a nondescript poet in a
Tantalizing image on the outskirts of your retina.

A VOICE
> *Our sense it is of wonder and mistake—*
> *Cells in the open eye-stalk of the brain*
> *Become a lens of crystal-fibre grain,*
> *With pencilled light its focal point to make.*
>
> *Pre-fissured for the missing speck, the break*
> *Remains unclosed; the eye cannot attain*
> *The perfect circle of the normal strain.*
> *So, "Did the Hand then of the Potter shake?"*
>
> *One cell was tardy in the saraband,*
> *Its late appointed partner had moved on,*
> *Now never will it grasp the waiting hand.*
>
> *A blindly wondrous dance, or marathon,*
> *But why so irremediably "planned"?*
> *"For ever wilt thou love, and she be gone!"*

NARRATOR
Ah, not a puzzle or a satire, but a *thought*!
Whereas the once respected Paley taught
That God is an infallible artificer
Too perfect (or insensitive) to err,

It now appears that He, so humanly divine,
Allows blind Chance to mess up his design!
(It's incidentally clear that one who versicle attempts on
A tricky theme like this must be a follower of E-----).

A VOICE
    The patient's temperature is normal,
    His pulse-beat is regular both in rhythm and in force,
    But examination reveals slight paroxysmal tachycardia
    With extra-systolic palpitations.
    He has since passed into a heavy trance,
    Bordering at times on complete unconsciousness.
    Indications, however, are consistent,
    Not, as has been suggested,
    With conine poisoning,
    (In which event his brain would have remained
       unclouded throughout,
    As in the classic case of Socrates),
    But with the effects of belladonna,
    Hyoscine, or other alkaloid narcotic,
    For there now succeed symptoms of delirium,
    Utterances of a disjointed character,
    Relating in particular to some arboreal, mytho-
       ornithological hybrid
    Suffering from an estival fixation
    And an euphoric-eupeptic-hedonistic obsession—
    Concluding with an extraordinary statement
    As to the sufficiency of merely aesthetic evaluations
    As a basis of behaviour—
    All of the order of oneiristic, schismatical, polytheistic
       hallucination.
    The patient has been given an emetic
    And his stomach has been washed out with saline,

*And he should henceforth be insulated from all harmful
    stimuli,
Such as objects that are in any way beautiful,
Sounds that are in any way harmonious,
And ideas that are in any way original, plausible, liberal,
    or inspiring,
And his reading-matter should be limited to
The Daily Sketch and the works of Sir Arnold Lunn.
He is obviously in a disturbed psychological condition,
But considering that the data point to
A pagan upbringing
Rather than to the ordinary social or occupational
    neuroses
Of our contemporary civilization,
I feel that his case should be referred,
Not to a psychiatrist or psychoanalyst,
But to the resident chaplain of the hospital.*

NARRATOR
What is this monstrosity, this parody, this "stumer"?
What is this heavy piece of undergraduate humour?
Nothing of the sort, you say, a labour of maturity,
Sponsored by the Ku Klux Klan, the Daughters of
    Mr Bowdler, and the C-th-lic League of Purity,
Part of a world-wide operation
To rid the literature of every nation
Of treason, colour, and temptation,
As well, of course, of all imagination.
Say what you like, I call it a disaster,
As bad as a Dickens Christmas "re-told" by Lady
    A----![1]

[1] It is not suggested that Lady A---- has actually "retold" a Dickens Christmas.

A VOICE

>*Orisons of the orgiastic Ebionite,*
>*Chuffed by the solid oxen of the Ghost,*
>*Mormed by the arthropods of malachite,*
>*And uffed by the Effluence of the Uttermost.*
>*Teleosts, dalmatics, gelignite, and toast,*
>*Uddered Usura, pustular and green,*
>*Boggling the spasms of the curdled coast:*
>*But pendulously posh, magniloquently mean,*
>*Fiffles the refulgence of the Pliocene.*
>
>*Insufferably sprog—...*

NARRATOR

The angry apparitions stamp and shout,
"Only a sacred cow could say what *that's* about."
"Where's the clumsy elephant's mahout?"
"Debag the blighter!" "Chuck him out!"

A VOICE

>*The Church Parade is good for discipline.*
>*If you invoke the Act and burn your boats*
>*You're a better man than I am, Gunga Din!*
>
>*The Major slowly sipped his second gin,*
>*The armoured Lancers feed their tanks on oats.*
>*The Church Parade is good for discipline.*
>
>*You saw the Pope's encyclical on sin*
>*Where "God is Love" appears in double "quotes"?*
>*You're a better man than I am, Gunga Din.*
>
>*Your trigger-happy generals cannot win*
>*For modern castles all have useless moats.*
>*The Church Parade is good for discipline.*

Unless you put your gun in vaseline,
Land's End will be on top of John o' Groats.
You're a better man than I am, Gunga Din!

Now keep your fingers off the safety-pin
And let United Nations have your votes.
The Church Parade is good for discipline;
You're a better man than I am, Gunga Din!

NARRATOR
    A youthful voice from somewhere near the skylight,
    And though his figure hovers in the twilight,
    He seems to be an officer in battle-dress.
    The subject of his poem, I should guess,
    Is random conversation in the Mess.
    But what's his regiment? A bolshie lot,
    I'd say, whose fighting spirit's gone to pot—
    Pale-pink defeatists, talking tommy rot,
    For (it's common knowledge) "We have got
    The Maxim gun and they have not."

        But listen, I hear the Chorus
           Tuning their silent drum
        To conjure up from Time's abysm
           The Shape of Things to Come.

           CHORUS
    Life is earnest, life is raw
    We must take it on the jaw
    When lesser breeds without the law
    Purloin our base at Singapaw.[1]

---

[1] Spelling to meet Mr Graves's Celtic scruples regarding rhyme.

Art lies mangled in the maw
Of Business red in tooth and claw
The bishops croak, the poets caw
Grand Opera is Mammon's squaw.

Since you can neither paint nor draw
You'll sell your pictures by the scaw[1]
Your verse would make an old macaw
Utter an impolite guffaw.

Exit Laski, Wells, and Shaw
Enter Toynbee, Greene, and Waugh
While the grim wolf with privy paw
Devours the sheep in Arkansas.

A VOICE
  Mr Narrator, what we have heard so far are the
     jugglers and the acrobats of Letters,
  Mere contortionists who mock or parody their betters.
  Has this poor age no star to fill the void?
  Have we no Harry Lauder, Little Tich, or Marie
     Lloyd?

NARRATOR
  Ladies and gentlemen, be patient please,
  Tonight's performance has no unities,
  No acts, no scenes, no plot, no choreography,
  No décor, theme, or any definite geography.
  The actors take the stage as suits their whim—
  But hark! I hear the distant tread of Him,
  Of Him, the Twentieth Century's undisputed Cham
  Of Poetry, and Britain's brightest gift from Uncle
     Sam!

[1] Spelling to meet Mr Graves's Celtic scruples regarding rhyme.

(There comes a hush:
All traffic stops from Russell Square to Shepherd's
  Bush.)

CHORUS
Who is he that cometh, like the flail of God,
With a frigid stare, as cold as any cod,
Riding 'neath a banner, inscribéd "Ichabod"?
Bard of Avon, this is he
Would have us think the less of thee.
Now to the roll of muffled drums
To us the fabled Sweeney comes.

II
SWEENEY IN ARTICULO

THE VOICE OF SWEENEY
    Sunday is the dullest day, treating
    Laughter as a profane sound, mixing
    Worship and despair, killing
    New thought with dead forms.
    Weekdays give us hope, tempering
    Work with reviving play, promising
    A future life within this one.
    Thirst overtook us, conjured up by Budweisserbrau
    On a neon sign: we counted our dollar bills.
    Then out into the night air, into Maloney's Bar,
    And drank whiskey, and yarned by the hour.
    Das Herz ist gestorben,[1] swell dame, echt Bronx.
    And when we were out on bail, staying with the
        Dalai Lama,
    My uncle, he gave me a ride on a yak,
    And I was speechless. He said, Mamie,
    Mamie, grasp his ears. And off we went
    Beyond Yonkers, then I felt safe.
    I drink most of the year and then I have a Vichy.

      Where do we go from here, where do we go,
    Out of the broken bottles? Pious sot!
    You have no guide or clue for you know only
    Puce snakes and violet mastodons, where the brain
        beats,
    And a seltzer is no answer, a vomit no relief,
    And the parched tongue no feel of water. Only
    There is balm in this YMCA

(Claim now the balm inside this YMCA),
And you will see that there is more in life than
Those vigils at the doors of pubs in the morning,
Or bootings from the doors of pubs at closing-time.
I will show you fear in a pile of half-bricks.
> *Wer reitet so spät*
> *Durch Nacht und Wind?*
> *Es ist der Vater mit seinem Kind.*[2]

"You called me 'Baby Doll' a year ago;
  You said that I was very nice to know,"
Yet when we came back late from that Wimbledon
  dance-hall,
Your arms limp, your hair awry, you could not
Speak, and I likewise, we were neither
Living nor dead, and we knew nothing,
Gazing blankly before us in the carriage.
"Bank Station! All change! *Heraus! Heraus!*"

   (Cloax is the vilest drink, gouging
Pockets out of your giblets, mixing
Frenzy and remorse, blending
Rot-gut and white-ants.
Jalap has a use, laundering
Colons with refreshing suds, purging
The lower soul with gentle motion.)

   Count Cagliostro,[3] famous impostor,
Often in gaol, nevertheless
Enjoyed a great career, adored by the ladies.
Sold them love and youth elixirs. Said he,
Take this powder, "Lymph of Aphrodite",
("In delay there lies no plenty."[4] See!)
Made with belladonna, that lightens up your eyes,
Enhances your fascinations.

Much more than this, now listen, it gives you power
To peep into the past and future, crystalline bright.
Just a pinch, you witness the fall of ancient Troy,
Another small pinch, a deep breath, before your eyes
The Apocalypse! Just watch *me* taste.
Lo! The Four Horsemen and the Beast, as plain as the stars!
Goodbye, Marquise. If you see her Majesty the Queen,
Tell her I have the Diamond Necklace,[5]
It's hidden in my *cabinet de toilette*.

    Earthly Limbo,
Chilled by the raw mist of a January day,
A crowd flowed down King's Parade, so ghostly,
Mowed down by the centuries, so ghostly.
You barely heard the gibbering and the squeaks
As each man gazed in front with staring eyes,
Flowed past Caius Insurance Offices
To where the clock in Trinity Great Court
Marked off the hours with male and female voice.
There I saw one I knew, and hailed him shouting,
    Muravieff-Amursky!
You who were with me up at Jesus,
And fought in my battalion at Thermopylae!
Your brain-box stopped an arrow, you old cadaver.
Are you Hippolytus,[6] killed by your horses' hoofs,
Revivified by Aesculapius?
"I sometimes think there never blows so red
  The Rose as where some buried Caesar bled."[7]
"If Winter comes can Spring be far behind?"[8]

NARRATOR
    His words are very indistinct—perhaps it's atmospherics?

He's quoting from the *Daily Telegraph,* and now
  there's a piece that sounds as if it might be
  Herrick's—
Ah, there he is once more, completely audible again,
Summing up his views, I think, though he seems to be
  in pain!

THE VOICE OF SWEENEY
  This is the vacant mind,
  This is the barren mind,
  Empty, bereft of intellect,
  Can nothing fill the yawning void?
  Is there no voodoo, charm, or pious platitude
  To save the world from thought?
  . . . . .
  But you must believe in *something*!
  Can't you see it's only *allegor*ical!
  And what would happen to society?
  . . . . .
  *Iudica me, Deus, et discérne causam meam de gente non
    sancta: ab hómine iníquo, et dolóso érue me.*⁹
  Boomalay, boomalay, boomalay, boom!¹⁰
  *L'Érèbe les eût pris pour ses coursiers funèbres,*¹¹
  聖人因而興制不事心焉¹²

  𓁷𓏤𓈖𓏏𓀀𓅓𓅱𓎛¹³
  ... --- ...¹⁴
  𓂝𓏤𓄿𓅓𓋴¹⁵
  "Love thy neighbour as thyself,"
  "Couldn't you bring better weather with
    you?" and,
  Above all,
  "Please adjust your dress before leaving."¹⁶
  . . . .

63

Up and down the City Road
In and out the "Eagle",
That's the way the money goes,
Pop, goes the weasel.

. . . . .

*Aspérges me Dómine hyssópo, et mundábor; lavábis me
et super nivem dealbábor.*[17]

Eeny, meeny, miney mo,
Catch a nigger by his toe,
By his toe,
      Miney mo
     -ney mo
       o!

This is what the curate said,
This is what the curate said,
This is what the curate said,
  Not with a fart but a simper.

NOTES

[1] Schiller, *Des Mädchens Klage*.

[2] Goethe, *Erlkönig*.

[3] Count Cagliostro (1743–95), Italian alchemist, whose real name was Giuseppe Balsamo. (See Note 5 below.)

[4] Shakespeare, *Sweet and Twenty*.

[5] The Affair of the Diamond Necklace (1778–86). A mysterious incident which involved Marie Antoinette. In the sensational trial which ensued, Cagliostro was acquitted.

Here Cagliostro figures as the Prophet of the Age of Unreason, which he foretold would begin in earnest in 1922.

[6] Hippolytus, son of Theseus by Hippolyta, Queen of the Amazons. He was falsely suspected of having attempted the dishonour of Theseus' second wife, Phaedra. Poseidon, at the instigation of Theseus, sent forth a bull from the water at which the horses drawing Hippolytus' chariot took fright, overturned the chariot, and dragged Hippolytus along the ground until he was dead. Artemis, however, induced Aesculapius to restore him to life again.

Originally a Vegetation Myth, but here, for the sake of poetical consistency, Aesculapius administers arsenic instead of elixir to Hippolytus.

[7] FitzGerald, *Omar Khayyám*. "The Rose"=Pernicious Anaemia.

[8] Shelley, *Ode to the West Wind*. For "Winter" read "Spring" and vice versa.

[9] Roman Catholic *Liturgy of the Mass*. Here read in Anglican (or "Pickwickian") sense.

[10] Vachel Lindsay, *The Congo*. Last words of St Mumbo Jumbo.

[11] Baudelaire, *Les Chats*. Euphony only (no relevance).

[12] From *Lü Shih Ch'un Ch'iu*. "The Sage follows Nature in establishing social order, and does not invent principles out of his own head."
Since this is a rational statement in authentic Chinese it is thought to have slipped in by mistake for a quotation from Mr Pound.

[13] From an ancient Egyptian inscription. Literally, "Thy breath of life is sweet in my nostril."
"Life" here is an occult symbol for death.

[14] The famous Morse signal of distress sent out by the *Titanic* on 14 April 1912. Here it is sent out by the inhabitants of the "Unreal City". No one answers it.

[15] "Hydor", water, short for "Ariston Men Hydor", i.e. "Take more water with it." A message in manual code from Microcephalos, the deaf-and-dumb soothsayer of Thebes, to Tiresias (who was blind anyway) on the morning after a feast. Here it signifies the Seven Types of Ambiguity.

[16] Reproduced by permission of the Westminster City Council.

[17] *Liturgy of the Mass*. See Note 9 above.

"The Vacant Mind" contains allusions and adaptations from thirty-five different writers in twenty languages, including Pali, Sanskrit, Aramaic, Tagálog, Swahili, and Bêche-de-mer.

NARRATOR

We thank you, Sir, you are most kind
To read us extracts from your masterpiece, "The Vacant Mind",
The poem that revolutionized the poet's point of view
Way back in '22.
Once more you lower your trajectory,
Exploding harmless shells in vicarage and rectory,
And causing piddling thrills in college and refectory.
"What does it mean?" Here's someone says he knows,
But asks our leave to spread himself in prose.

A VOICE

"The Vacant Mind", Mr Narrator, stands for the present empty age in which there is a catastrophic clash between the Old Tradition and the New Heresy. The Dalai Lama is the Archbishop of Canterbury, and to stay at Lambeth is the acme of social ambition. The yak is the local bloodstock to bestride which gives a *panache* to the mere artisan of letters. The YMCA stands for the highest aseptic morality and for the chilly welcome of the Church of England. The London Underground is (needless to say) Inferno itself and the Bank Station marks the entry to the bottommost pit reserved for "sinners by malice", poets like Shelley, "little upstarts" like Hobbes, most non-Anglicans (except RCs), and those, such as Bernard Shaw, Lord Russell, Dag Hammarskjöld, Sir Alexander Fleming, Paul Ehrlich, and Florence Nightingale, who retain some hope for the human race and for a bearable life on earth. "Ancient Troy" is the modern megalopolis (London, Paris, etc.) whose fall is correctly foreseen by Cagliostro's client, albeit through the agency of the impostor's powder. The Apocalypse is the Apocalypse. The Diamond Necklace represents Mammon, Jews, and Bradford millionaires, and the *cabinet de toilette* all the loathsome functions of the human body, especially sex. "Caesar" stands in reverent substitution for a Holier Name. The "Rose" is the miracle of the Sacrament. "Winter" is the barrenness of today, and "Spring" is the brave old world in which the *Civitas Dei* will be restored and reinforced, sanitation will be abolished and disease reinstated, wherein the hierarchy will be more powerful than ever it was in the past, and wherein a bigger and better Inquisition will burn all books included on a greater and grander Index and will consign heretics wholesale to the flames.

NARRATOR

    Thank you for a pretty piece of exegesis
    In perfect concord with the Sweeney thesis.
    But other critics have construed the text,
    Each one in terms quite different from the next,
    And each one's version of the sense
    In equal keeping with the evidence.
    One holds that "Caesar" is the late-lamented Führer,
    The "Rose", his doctrine, now upper-class and purer,
    Another says that Con is Phlebas fished up from Davy
        Jones's Locker,
    A third insists that Hip is Scorpio: another swears he's
        Lady Docker.
    With suchlike shufflings of the Tarot pack
    Through all the phases of the Zodiac,
    For Sweeney—friar, hermit, yogi, and vedantist,
    Our greatest poet-obscurantist,
    Has most adroitly fixed it so—
    Omne ignotum pro magnifico![1]

    But be his spirit white or black or be it pied,
    Be his writing honoured or decried,
    One fact remains that cannot be denied—
    That (unofficially at least) the Blessed Sweeney is
        beatified.
    His cult is authorized in person or by proxy
    By all the cardinals and priests, the ruling laity, and the
        acolytes of orthodoxy,
    And one shouldn't be surprised
    If, when he's dead, he's forthwith canonized.

---

[1] "Have you guessed the riddle yet?" the Hatter said, turning to Alice again. "No, I give it up," Alice replied: "What's the answer?"
"I haven't the slightest idea," said the Hatter.
"Nor I," said the March Hare.
    Alice sighed wearily. "I think you might do something better with the time," she said, "than waste it asking riddles with no answer."

A VOICE

Mr Narrator, in view of what you say, and considering the challenge offered by this arbitrary and unconstitutional procedure on the part of the hierarchy to the independence and sovereignty of the great Republic of Letters,

Which only a few centuries ago freed itself—at least nominally—from being the handmaiden of the Church and from suchlike ecclesiastical fetters,

May I suggest that you refer the matter on our behalf to the Literary Assembly

When next it meets on Helicon, at the British Council, or in the Stadium at Wembley,

Expressing our unanimous conviction

That the mundo-heavenly Establishment has gone beyond its jurisdiction,

Usurping the Republican Tribunal,

Letters, we hold, are not sacred but commúnal,

Insisting that a writer should receive his meed of praise

Not as a halo but a crown of bays.

NARRATOR

Well said! Your motion, Sir, is carried with acclaim,
The Public, not the Clericals, shall be the arbiters of Sweeney's fame.
But in order that we may clarify our views upon this question,
I would make the following suggestion.
Let us pretend we are a Papal Congregation,
Convened to adjudicate on Sweeney's elevation,
To scan his inspiration on heroic level
And say if he be moved by God or Devil.
X, the famous critic, shall be Postulator,

Y, the Devil's Advocate, the "Pope"—why, your
Narrator!

(The shadowy audience, filled with ghostly glee,
Eerily cheer to show that they agree).

THE "POPE"
Your lordships, acting Cardinals, we'll try this cause
Not by priestly, but by humanistic laws.
We are not gods, our Sweeney we will scan
As poet, critic, sociologist, and man.
And though I am your pontiff and your oracle,
You'll please remember this is only metaphorical.
We'll deal in good and evil, not in "grace" and "sin".
Now, Mr Postulator, will you please begin?

POSTULATOR
May it please your Holiness, I will open my case for my client, the saintly—and, I hope, to be sanctified—Sweeney, by asking you to recall the state of affairs that existed in England at the close of the First World War.

Four years of conflict had destroyed the old social values and had resulted in universal emptiness and disillusionment. The great tradition of the past was irrevocably broken, faith had declined, the class system was cracked, and the result was a cultural void. On the upper level, to adopt my client's symbolism, "Women do their hair, copying the paintings of Vermeer," and the merely rich had succeeded to the bankrupt inheritance of the Edwardian Establishment, rooted firmly as it had been in the Catechism, untaxed investment, and Marienbad; and on the lower level there were "one-night cheap hotels", shambling waiters with their dirty love affairs, old men drooling at the mouth, and serving-maids with humid souls—all the squalid exudations of a modern megalopolis and the horrors of an egalitarian world. Pandering to the ambitions of the masses was exemplified in the popular slogans of the time—"The War to End Wars", "To Make the World Safe for Democracy", and in the organizations designed to bring Utopia on earth, such as The League of Nations, the Society for the Abolition of Flogging, the NSPCC, the RSPCA, and the like. Furthermore, the newly rich, who might in time have re-established the Old Order, were crippled by taxation to provide bonuses for the ex-service men now swarming back like rabbits to these shores, while the industrial proletariat was voicing demands for privileges that in the Victorian-Edwardian period of British greatness would have been unthinkable.

In the field of literature, the long classical succession had come to an end and no new one had arisen to take its place. The war itself had produced few poets worthy of the name, and these few had usually chosen to express themselves in outworn forms and metres. From whence could salvation come? Scarcely, it seemed, from within the country, since the youth of Britain who had survived the war were busy trying to pick up the threads of a vanished life or, now that service pay had stopped, were absorbed in a struggle for a livelihood. It was, for the sensitive onlooker, a time of cultural futility and spiritual despair.

CHORUS

The howitzers are dumb,
    The dead (at best) are numb,
The willow-warblers sing
    In the ruins of Elverdinghe,
But here there is no hope
    Except in a length of rope.

It is at this critical and decisive juncture that the blessed Sweeney arrives on the scene. A neutral for most of the war and rejected for the American Navy in its last stages, he had become imbued with an admiration for the British social system, so resistant to reform yet so skilful in transmuting new wealth into ancient aristocracy. Standing aloof, he is immune from the emotions of the young men in uniform, or just out of it. Thus he can see things with a fresh eye and hear things with a fresh ear. Nor is he influenced by the prevailing mood of shallow optimism reflected in the slogan, "A Land fit for Heroes to live in". To use his own words, "In a world of self-determination, electoral reform, plebiscites, sex reform, slum-clearance, venereal clinics, old-age pensions, and universal education, the possibility of damnation is an immense relief, for, in the midst of this horrible meliorist boredom it gives at least a significance to life." The one hope lies in the resurrection of traditional values, in the re-establishment of Original Sin, the primacy of Church and Throne, and Classicism in Letters. But in this last regard, reverence for the pure models of the Reverend John Donne, Bishop Lancelot Andrewes, and Dr Johnson must be accompanied by a revolution in reverse—and it is Sweeney, the American scholar steeped in European learning, who, both as poet and critic, is chosen by the Divine Will to make it.

CHORUS
Burn down the hospitals; we shall not cry,
    Fill in the drains; we have no sense of smell;
Let wealth and commerce, laws and learning die,
    But leave—Oh, leave us still our hope of Hell!

Sweeney at an early stage in his career stated his credo which he has subsequently amended and modified, but from the main principles of which he has not departed. A poet, he held, must be of the Tradition, of the Main Current, of the Established Order, of Things as they Are—or rather Were. He must have a deep historical sense and yet have his own generation in his bones. Expression in English poetry had gone wrong, had become out of date because it had lost its relationship with the common speech. Between poetry and the common speech there must be an enduring connexion, and each poetic revolution has inevitably involved a return to the colloquial forms of the day. By "common", of course, my client did not mean "vulgar" speech or provincial dialect. One of the least contaminated survivals of the English tradition was the language of the cultivated élite of the nation (who never, by the way, figure directly in Sweeney's poems but are always behind the scenes) spoken in its limpid purity in the salons of Mayfair and Belgravia, in country mansions, and, *in excelsis*, in the Anglican pulpit. This must be the basis of a reformed and revivified verse.

It was out of an overwhelming sense of the vileness and emptiness of contemporary existence and its crushing boredom that "The Vacant Mind" was conceived. It is the "Vacant Mind" of the mass civilization; the sick mind thirsting unconsciously for a salvation which can come to it only through sacrifice. The "sacrifice" called for is not the facile sacrifice of death in battle, but the sacrifice of human allurements and relationships, of earthly "love", of sensual pleasure, of reproduction, and of the deluding pretence that man is "basically decent"—as the cant of the time expresses it. This is the insidious neo-Pelagianism of the nineteen-twenties. Sweeney, in his first great poem, expresses the agony of despair of the God-aspiring soul in a world without belief.

Likewise, "The Vacant Mind" is the record *par excel-*

lence of the soul-disintegrating collision in a sensitive mind of the Old Tradition and the new heresy of Science and Modern Learning. Fragments of the Old Morality survive in dualistic contrast with pieces of the intruding heresy in the débris of the ruin. This confusion of elements becomes the pattern of Sweeney's poem. Recollections of the collapsed culture lie cheek by jowl with the passing crazes of the day in the confusion of seeming accident. Passages or phrases from Shakespeare or Webster, Donne or Traherne, alternate with the jetsam of politics or jazz, vapid chatter, popular science, and gutter journalism.

But while the fabric of the "Unreal City", the metropolis of "The Vacant Mind", is paved with the abrasion of the old and the new, with city garbage and the effulgence of "The Word", Sweeney's poem is a most ingenious and orderly contrivance. He has resorted to anthropology to give point to his theme—but has turned it inside out and upside down to suit his higher purposes. In the ancient vegetation myths sex assumes a universal or religious significance: it is connected with the state of the land. The cycle of the seasons is a divinely ordered series of events, and the procession of life is based on sex and personified in ritualistic figures. One of these, the Fisher King, was castrated and magically restored to potency. Water, in primitive belief, was the life-giving element: in Sweeney it is "The Word". Whereas in the Vegetation Myth the spring is a renewal of life, a season of rejoicing, in "The Vacant Mind" it is the season of frustration and despair. The people in the poem are not made happy by the return of spring and the fruitfulness of the soil; they prefer the barrenness of winter, the dead and holy season. And whereas sex in primitive belief is associated with generation and elevated thereby into the imaginative conception of "love" on the human level, in Sweeney's poem it is a degrading lust which can be sublimated only by faith into the spiritual Divine Life, for in the words of St John of the Cross, "the soul cannot be possessed of divine union until it has divested itself of the love of created beings." (The sexual, or homo-sexual, imagery used by St John is, it seems, a necessary stage in this purification.) The fertility of the Vegetation Myth is thus excised from "The Vacant Mind" as a heresy and an illusion, which makes it perhaps the purest poem in the English language. Throughout the poem there is the weight of the threat of impending new dark ages. The ecstasy of the soul is lost when cut off from the roots of faith.

CHORUS
Behold the eunuch Fisher King,
A poor denatured clod,
Powerless to procreate the spring
Out of the winter sod,
A sacrificial offering
To the anti-sex of God.

It is not easy, your Holiness, to interpret the sense of this most complex and subtle poem, and indeed there have been complaints on all sides of its obscurity. But as the saintly Sweeney himself has declared, "It is never what a poem *says* that matters, but what it *is*." And indeed "The Vacant Mind" is more of an incantation than a tract. The essence of an "indirect" poem is that it cannot be pinned down to precise meanings. It is protean in form, and directly it is in danger of being identified by the gross apprehensions of the ordinary reader as, shall we say, your Holiness, a horse, it turns into a turkey or a sheep. It is all things to all men; not a mere factual statement. Sweeney says, "The more seasoned reader does not bother about understanding—not, at least, at first." As a distinguished literary critic puts it, "Take care of the sounds and the sense will take care of itself."

But while my client rebukes those who would search for a meaning and refuse to enjoy a poem for its own sake, he makes it clear that it should nevertheless not be devoid of significant content: it must be written "according to definite religious and moral standards and from a definite theological viewpoint". What it all amounts to is that while Sweeney's poems are definitely religious in an oblique way, they are as unsubmissive to reduction to prose-logic as are the Psalms, and the critic who would shrink from attempting to render down, "My soul is among lions: I lie even among them that are set on fire" into ordinary everyday English must pause equally before analysing the symbolism of "The Vacant Mind".

Sweeney at this juncture was convinced of the universal moral bankruptcy of society, of the breakdown of the culture, and of the hollowness of the land of his adoption. Yet already he saw the glimmerings of a way out—through the Church of England, purged of its modernism and restored to its pre-Reformation state, and through asceticism and celibacy which are more blessed than marriage and in which sensual enjoyment is sublimated into a thirst for "The Word".

CHORUS
Wrapt in the old miasmal mist,
    Embedded in a secret code,
The mystery of the Eucharist
    Lurks in the strophe and the ode.

> Osiris and the Golden Fleece,
>   The ritual of the Sterile Seed,
> The lore of Egypt and of Greece,
>   Sugar the Athanasian Creed.
>
> The magic of a pagan name,
>   Poor Ovid's misery condign,
> In deep obliquity proclaim,
>   "The Articles are Thirty-Nine."

POSTULATOR
  I wish to protest, your Holiness, against the intervention of the Chorus.
  For one thing, my client and I find it very hard to decide when it's against us and when it's for us.
  In any case it's not impartial in its bearing
  And its only object seems to be to prejudice the hearing.

THE "POPE"
  I fear, in this regard, I'm quite without authority,
  The supernatural beings whom we hear but cannot see
  Provide a non-judicial commentary—
  Dryads or sylphs, perhaps, or Demogorgon,
  Angels and furies, a choir without an organ—
  Which does not enter in the pleadings
  And forms no part of the proceedings.
  Moreover, it appears,
  Its songs mean different things to different ears,
  Just as you say your client's do—
  It all depends upon your point of view.

POSTULATOR

As your Holiness pleases.

The poetic progress of Sweeney has been logical and inevitable. It has run parallel to a spiritual progress from an agony of despair to the reality of belief. Sweeney has always insisted on the necessity of "doubt" as a stage towards belief, but it must not be the rationalist scepticism which ignores revelation as not worthy of serious thought, but the "doubt" of a Pascal which exists only to be overcome. He *wishes* to believe but has to torture his intellect into submission before he can satisfy the cravings of his soul. In the same way Sweeney rejoices in the Satanism and Black Mass of Baudelaire as "faith by paradox", while he recoils from the facile belief of Tennyson who, like a Chinese Buddhist, visualizes the next world as a kind of continuation of this earthly life. Sweeney refuses to conceive eternity in any concrete or worldly terms so that it remains increate, amorphous, and undefined—not even as realized as Vaughan's "ring of endless light". Life has a meaning only as a preparation for death. "Life is very long," he laments, but the believer is not permitted the self-indulgence of suicide.

His next long poem, "The Bloodbath of the Mass", marks a definite step forward in Sweeney's poetic career. It is a magnificent tract in the form of a paraphrase of the Roman Catholic Liturgy, in which quotations from the *Ave Maria*, the *Salve Regina*, the *Canon of the Mass*, and the *Anima Christi* make up ninety per cent of the whole. The same theme is repeated in the incantations of his later poem, "Colney Hatch". The Prayer to the Virgin in "The Last Vestíges", incidentally, is not "Mariolatry", as has been suggested by Sweeney's critics, but poetic licence. In this latter poem Sweeney abandons Webster and Marlowe as quarries for his tesserae and turns to

Robert Montgomery, Mrs Hemans, Ella Wheeler Wilcox, and Martin Tupper, and, since these poets are little remembered nowadays, the effect achieved is one of almost complete originality. "The immature poet imitates: the mature poet steals," says Sweeney; but the artful poet learns to cover up his tracks.

In his later poems the saintly Sweeney has brought out the disorder, the futility, the meaninglessness, the whole horror, bestiality, and boredom of modern life. "Vanity of Vanities, all is Vanity, saith the Preacher," and from this condemnation only the Church, the Throne, and the Cultural élite are exempted.

CHORUS

Ah, what avails the sceptred race,
    Ah, yes, and what the form divine?—
Gesture of orang-outang,
    Shambling, hairy, human swine.

Sound, sound, the clarion, fill the fife,
    Throughout the sensual world proclaim,
Polyphiloprogenitive,
    Eve's mistake and Adam's shame.

Heap cassia, sandalbuds, and stripes
    Of labdanum, and aloe balls;
Smother the smell of bodies vile,
    Urinals, drains, and cockle-stalls.

Curs'd be the shade of Percy Bysshe,
    Unwept, unhonoured, and unsung;
Tobacco gives eternal life
    By way of cancer of the lung.

>   "Love is a many-splendoured thing"—
>   Raving of heresiarch!
>   The Saints bemoan the growing pile
>   Of contraceptives in the park.

I shall not, your Holiness, take up the time of this sacred Congregation in describing the excellencies of the saintly Sweeney's plays as I have his major poems, but if I were to do so I should present him in a rôle in which he equally merits the *fame* of blessedness. Even those passages in them which have reminded profane critics of the *ABC* or *Whitaker's Almanac* contain hidden wisdom as deep as anything in his poems. The world had already hailed him as the greatest poet of our time. Has not the august British Council declared that "He may speak for English letters with the voice of authority"? Has he not been proclaimed the "Literary Loyola of the Modern Age"? Though it may sound premature for me to say so, I am confident that this sacred Congregation will consider him worthy of an even greater honour. Indeed, I can already hear the solemn mass of the *Veni Creator* in the triumphant tones of the litany of canonization.

THE "POPE"
>   Thank you, Mr X. Without a doubt a masterly
>   address,
>   If I may say so, a model of forensic exposition,
>   nothing more or less.
>   But in order that the Court
>   Shall not get muddled in its thought,
>   We'll take the cause by sections. We have heard
>   The plaintiff's claim to be preferred
>   To bardic sanctity.
>   I call on the Promotor Fidei,
>   On this one point to comment on his plea.

DEVIL'S ADVOCATE

May it please your Holiness.

At the very outset of my rebuttal of the eloquent plea of my learned friend, your Holiness, I would make it clear to this sacred Congregation that I have no personal knowledge of the Claimant whatever and speak of him only from the evidence of his published writings.

Let me acknowledge at once that "The Vacant Mind" is a landmark in English poetry, and that its influence, for good or for evil, is seen in the writings of nearly every poet since it appeared. Moreover, the workmanship of the Claimant's early verse revealed him as a master craftsman, while the versatility of his scholarship cannot be denied. At the same time, I submit, your Holiness, that his reputation has been largely established and magnified by interests unconnected with poetry and for reasons which have nothing to do with the quality of his verse. I aim to prove that Sweeney, a minor poet who might otherwise have escaped extensive notice, has, for motives altogether hostile to the spirit of literature, been elevated by vested interest into his present exalted position. He has received every honour the Establishment has to bestow; the cathedrals of England have acquired a new lease of life as theatres for his plays; and even philistines whose houses are furnished with hundred-guinea TV sets (and no books) glow with a vague but dutiful approval at the mention of his name.

My learned friend has invited the Court to visualize the state of affairs in England immediately after the First World War. He has described the universal disillusionment and emptiness out of which "The Vacant Mind" took shape. Now, it happens that I belong to the generation which fought this war, and so, if I am not mistaken, does your Holiness. The prevailing sentiment among those who had survived the war certainly bears no resemblance to that depicted in "The Vacant Mind". Those of us who were still in one piece were delighted—if surprised. The tragedy as we saw it was not the collapse of a culture, but the abominable wastefulness of war which had slaughtered the flower of British manhood and breeding-stock and had thus condemned Britain to become a second-class nation in the foreseeable future. The singer of "The Vacant Mind" was concerned with none of these things. The sacrifice and the slaughter had left him indifferent. The only reference to the war and its million dead in "The Vacant Mind" is to the false teeth of the wife of a "demobbed" soldier!

Detachment may be a virtue, your Holiness, but we should not applaud the person who, happening by some accident to be present at the Crucifixion, looks the other way and goes on doodling with his stilus or brooding over his purely personal miseries.

Has Sweeney not declared that "We must learn to suffer more"? And that he spoke in no purely mental or moral sense is proved by his statement—"I have no more sympathy with the purely humanitarian attitude towards war than the humanitarian attitude towards anything else: I should not enjoy the prospect of abolishing suffering without at the same time perfecting human nature." In other words, he is content to see blood-baths indefinitely repeated to satisfy the thirst of that insatiable Moloch whom he calls his "God".

CHORUS
"And who will vindicate our absent sons?"
"Only the monstrous anger of the guns."
"Mr Palethorpe, will you kindly pass the buns?"

The preoccupations of the youth of England who had survived the war were very different from those of the denizens of the "Unreal City" of which Sweeney had made himself a citizen. They wished to make up for lost time and to get on with the business of living and, if possible, to make sure that wars did not happen again. When Sweeney wrote "The Vacant Mind", the Versailles Peace had not yet failed and the "Great Slump" was still many years ahead. The war itself had resulted in a very great improvement in the living conditions of the working classes—a matter of no concern to the Claimant, as the whole tone of his writings demonstrates. The emptiness and disillusionment of "The Vacant Mind" was not, I submit, the emptiness and disillusionment of contemporary Britain, but the exclusive personal problem of the unreal inhabitants of Sweeney's "Unreal City".

The tactful omission of the war was naturally appreciated in protected circles, but it was not only the *embusqués* who were attracted to Sweeney. By an irony, many of the young men who had missed the war because of their youth were pleased to forget it for quite different reasons. They felt cheated of their taste of glory as the lame boy in the "Pied Piper" felt that he had been cheated of the paradise (?) that lay at the other side of the mountain.

It is a curious fact that persons of the same type were attracted to both Sweeney and D. H. Lawrence. The two men could scarcely have been more dissimilar—the former exalted chastity and asceticism: the latter made a god of sex; Lawrence scorned the social conventions that Sweeney revered. The one thing they offered in common, your Holiness, was escape from reality. Sweeney offered it in the form of a kind of gloomy maze set up in the Vicarage garden for the Church bazaar; Lawrence offered vicarious virility to those who by reason of flat-feet, varicose veins, or other disability had been selected to live. But whereas Sweeney was willing to fight when his country ceased to be neutral, Lawrence, who suffered from tuberculosis, became almost hysterical with resentment when there was a chance of his being found fit for cannon-fodder. The two men agreed, however, in ignoring the great heroic drama and sombre tragedy of their generation. Sweeney, it seems, accepted the mass slaughter as a punishment of the human race for their sins: Lawrence regarded it as an irrelevance for his particular type of "superman".

The historically important fact about the two wars is statistical—namely that the best of the nation were removed before they had reproduced their species, and, as I understand biology,[1] this was a national loss that can never be repaired. Death is final and permits of no second thoughts. To meet the requirements of truth, the quotation from Julian Grenfell's poem must be amended to read:

"And who dies fighting has *no* increase."

Is, then, the type with the strongest "survival value" the one favoured by God or Nature? "Nature" has given its answer: if "God" confirms it, the victims who answered the call of the herd must be written off as contemptible dupes.

CHORUS

Strophe
>When Britain first at Heaven's command
>Said "No" to Kaiser Bill,
>My work and future were all planned,
>And I'd no wish to kill.

[1] Professor Bernal says in his *Science in History*, "It would be premature to claim that the methods of producing directed evolution have as yet succeeded." So "stock" still counts for something, even in Russia! M. B.

But when my friends put all at stake,
    And many paid the price,
I felt I could no longer make
    Vicarious sacrifice.

Despite my constitution frail
    And very doubtful sight,
The doctors all declared me hale
    And sent me out to fight.

Two years of war, then at Messines
    I stopped one with my head,
And now for forty years I've been
    Most well and truly dead.

A nihilistic infidel,
    I have myself to thank
That I am null and void as well,
    A sempiternal blank.

Antistrophe

    A scholar and a good athlete,
        At school I won the mile,
With youth to make my world complete
    I basked in fortune's smile.

Then came the war, a chance to cut
    A dash as hero fine.
I heard my country calling, but
    I felt I must decline.

A tremor in my runner's heart,
    A weakness at the knee,
Convinced me that a soldier's part
    Was not the one for me.

>   But when the Armistice came by
>   I felt a man reborn;
>   I rowed for my Leander tie
>   And climbed the Matterhorn.
>
>   Aged sixty-one, a fine career,
>   Six sons, a loving wife.
>   Reward, through faith, is coming near—
>   I'd rather stick to life!

Your Holiness may have been struck, as I have been, by the reluctance manifested by many of those professing faith in a future life to relinquish this worthless wordly one. This seems strangely inconsistent of them. Perhaps it is that while they possess faith, they lack confidence? It is in such noticeable contrast with the stoical acceptance of death on the part of many who have no expectation of a future life whatsoever.

> **CHORUS**
> " 'Condemned to life'?
>   Then why not risk it?"
> "What! Worms for bairns, the clammy earth for wife,
> This manly chest a piece of decomposing brisket?
>   You really take the biscuit!"

As one would suspect, Sweeney is not only out of sympathy but out of touch with the working classes. Who, for example, can imagine the British unemployed chanting, "No one has hired us! No one has hired us!" like a lot of sex-starved nanny-goats, as they do in his religious charade, "The Vault"? His social satire, too, misses the bus. It is like the cattishness of old women in a Kensington boarding-house—except when he gets on to the Jews; then he spits like a cheetah.

We cannot, I submit, your Holiness, gain a complete insight into Sweeney's character if we ignore the patronage and condescension which runs through his writings. A typical example is his remark, "We hope that the Italians will go on singing their operas superbly and producing excellent ice-creams." This sounds like a burlesque—but it seems that an alien by birth and upbringing cannot take on local colour without incurring some suspicion of self-satire. If the full implications of this are understood, I need spend no time in stressing Sweeney's partiality for General Franco, Marshal Pétain, or Charles Maurras, or for the banker-priest oligarchy of Europe and America. Sweeney, moreover, is utterly incapable of laughing at himself. But if he can't do it for himself, we shall have to do it for him.

CHORUS

In good King Edward's golden days,
When girls wore armour-plated stays,
Grand Opera was a ruling craze
    Approaching the fantastic.
While tenors clashed their tinny swords,
On Covent Garden's groaning boards
Sopranos flexed their vocal cords
    Like pieces of elastic.

When Tetrazzini touched top "C"
Or *bassos* reached the lower "B"
The house from stalls to gallery
    Applauded them like thunder.
Its notion of a soloist
Was one who could his in'ards twist—
A laryngeal contortionist
    Or vocal boneless-wonder.

But while these types from overseas,
Performing on the voice-trapeze,
Were paid enormous salaries
    And flattered to satiety,
Their lowly fellow-nationals
In floppy hats and patchwork shawls
Who ran the hoky-poky stalls
    Were outcasts of society.

The public bought their merchandise—
A wafer or a chocolate ice—
Because they sold it at a price
    Which suited their economy.
Their interest in the swarthy brave,
Who never seemed to have a shave
Between the cradle and the grave,
    All ended with gastronomy.

The English in these years of grace
Could not accord a serious place
Among the families of our race
    To the countrymen of Dante:
Regardless of their fame or means
Or dietary of tripe and beans,
They lumped them with the Argentines
    And the niggers of Ashanti.

The moral of this little tale
Is, where a native will not fail
To hide his foibles with a veil
    So others can't see through it,
An alien who adopts the stance
Of guileless English arrogance
And gazes down his nose askance
    Is bound to overdo it.

The 1914–18 war did not, as Sweeney holds, put an end to a flourishing condition of the arts. It is indeed a fantastic illusion to see the ethos of the age of which Edward VII and Sir Thomas Lipton were the symbols and the hobble-skirt and ragtime the acme of contemporary taste as a "culture" shattered by the cannon of Ypres or on the Somme. The musical echoes that sound through Sweeney's poems are not those of Alfred Austin, John Masefield, or William Watson, but of the great Elizabethans and the Metaphysicals. If any cultural edifice was brought down by the First World War it was that erected by Carlyle, Kipling, Marie Corelli, and Mr Podsnap—a collapse scarcely to be lamented. But the "hard-faced broker" civilization survived unimpaired, and was now reinforced by a vigorous army of war-profiteers. The stupid dead, who might have engineered a social and cultural renaissance, were not "on the job".

My learned friend has confined his claims for his client as a poet almost entirely to the two pieces which together form "The Vacant Mind", and wisely so. His later verse abandons the melody he owed to the incorporated echoes of the Renaissance lyricists and becomes a mere vehicle for conveying the formal doctrines of the Church.

Yeats it is who has said the last word on Sweeney as a singer. He speaks of his "flatness" and "monotony of accent", and concludes, "Nor can I put the Sweeney of those poems among those who descend from Shakespeare and the translators of the Bible. I think of him as a satirist rather than a poet." A well-known critic has spoken of Sweeney's "music of ideas": does he, may I ask, mean the tinkle of random reminiscences as played by the wind on an Aeolian harp?

"A poem is not what it *says*, but what it *is*." Perhaps so; perhaps not. The great poems of the past—*all* great poems of the past—have *said* something in addition to *being* something. That other great religious poem, "Jabberwocky", which is superficially unintelligible, was shown by Humpty Dumpty to have real significance. Apart from its borrowed echoes, "The Vacant Mind" is deliberately obscure, and it is only with the aid of Sweeney's prose writings (especially in out-of-the-way Church magazines) that we can attribute a plausible meaning to it, as did the anonymous critic who spoke before the convening of this Congregation.

To sum up, I have a feeling that Burke's reflections on the Chatham Administration of 1766-8, could, with small adaptations, be taken to describe "The Vacant Mind"—

> A poem so checkered and speckled with evocative phrases culled from the great poems of the past; a piece of joinery so crossly indented and whimsically dovetailed with pieces of ritual, myth, and anthropology; such a piece of diversified mosaic; such a tessellated pavement without cement, that it is indeed a curious show, but utterly unsafe to touch, and insecure to stand on.

Sweeney, I maintain, your Holiness, is a minor poet whose reputation, for reasons quite unconnected with poetry, has been inflated altogether beyond his merits until even the most sceptical of critics feels constrained to speak of him with bated breath and down his nose.

CHORUS
The curse of spring begins anew,
    Our miseries return,
Those lambs and crocuses, *eheu*!
    That we were ever born.
Heaven frowns, the sun's intrusive beam
Dissolves our cherished frozen dream.

How doth the dim religious bat
    Intoning in the dark
Or squeaking its magnificat
    Resent the joyous lark.
Zephyrs avaunt! but Boreas please
Rehearse your sad obituaries.

Thou, Chloris, must become a nun
    And leave thy godless cows,
And Lycius, the shepherd's son,
    Be bound by Trappist vows.
For spring and wickedness shall cease
When earth no longer has increase.

THE "POPE"
  A challenging indictment, Mr Y, couched in
    blistering invective—
  Or perhaps you'd rather have me say, "a salutary
    corrective
  To praise that was sometimes unselective".
  But we can only judge when we have heard the whole
  As to which of these assessments is the simulacrum of
    his soul.
  We've still to hear you gentlemen declaim
  Upon the sanctity of Sweeney's fame
  As wielder of a non-poetic logic
  In matters that are practical or pedagogic.
  Proceed, but for the comfort of the Court,
  I pray you make it short.

POSTULATOR
  While, your Holiness, the blessed-to-be Claimant was, in spite of the misrepresentations of my learned friend,

opening up new poetic horizons, he was, in his prose writings, accomplishing another silent revolution. His first concern was to do what Dr Johnson and Matthew Arnold had attempted in their time, namely to set the poets and the poems in a new order of merit according to the conceptions of the present age. In doing so he spoke (he said) "with the mind of Europe", a collective mind which, he points out, is more important than the private mind. This mind was that of the Great Tradition, the Establishment, which had persisted throughout the ages unaffected by revolutions, infidels, independent thinkers, and lawless powers. Sweeney puts Dante above Shakespeare, for the latter with his "mixed and muddled scepticism of the Renaissance" was "greater than his thought"; Milton he removes from his lofty pedestal; Burns, Shelley, and Keats are all but excluded from the Hall of Fame; while Dr Johnson is seen for the first time as a poet of the highest calibre. This, your Holiness, was undoubtedly a great feat and proves that my client is no respecter of persons—unless, of course, they are placed above criticism by their State or ecclesiastical function. Thanks to my client's reclassification, the textbooks on English literature have all had to be rewritten by members of the school that he has himself established.

In criticism, my saintly client's discovery of the "demonstrative deductive nominative", "the emotional insensitive", and the "insinuating oblique" have revolutionized the modern approach. One result of this is that scarcely a poem is written that can be pinned down to any one meaning—which ensures a great gain in variety. But all this is so well known to the present generation that I will not take up the time of the Court by elaborating it.

I now come to the saintly Sweeney's contribution to social and educational thought.

"Education has to be from top to bottom religious," he said in an article in a Church newspaper. The control of education, he went on, must be by priests and "the educational hierarchy should be a religious hierarchy." He advocated a strong reaction against the secularization of the universities, and recommended the reintroduction of the religious tests. Government, he said, should be conducted by those "whose responsibility is inherited with affluence and position". While careful to concede that education should be open to individuals with exceptional talent who have been properly "screened" and who are willing to swear allegiance to the Establishment, he insisted that it should be confined generally to the well-born and wealthy, "since to be educated above one's station leads to unhappiness and to social instability".

CHORUS
Neither liberal nor effete,
We're the cultural élite,
The issue of the Pulpit by the City.
"Reintroduce the past"
Is the motto of our caste
That's a cross between the Brahmin and the Chitty.[1]

We instigate the Press
To progressively regress,
Our grip upon the Bench is pretty thorough:
We've got our men of parts
As policemen of the arts;
The Foreign Office is our Pocket Borough.

To the future we are blind,
And we only look behind,
Our reverence is for Riches and Position,

[1] Hobson-Jobson for *Chettiar*, the Hindu money-lending caste.

> Despite our pin-stripe pants,
> We're only soft white-ants,
> The minions of the queen-termite, "Tradition".

The ideal at which the saintly Sweeney aimed is abundantly clear from his writings—namely the rule of the Church of Christ on earth. He considered that "tolerance was greatly overestimated." "I have no objection to being called a bigot myself," he declared. "The Church's business," he insisted, "was to *interfere* with the world": there could be no nonsense of "live and let live." It followed that a new Crusade, armed this time with atomic bombs, should forthwith be fitted out for the wholesale conversion of the Chinese, Indians, etc. who, with an insolence that could no more be tolerated than that of a Saladin, had recently asserted that, once and for ever, they refused to be saved. "If you want a Christian Society (he said) you cannot allow congeries of independent sects"; they must be eradicated. The Church, he added, has to speak "with final authority in moral matters and on the conduct of foreign affairs."

The saintly Sweeney was deeply aware that the culture of Europe was essentially Christian and lamented the retreat of Christianity before the advance of scientific paganism. "It is against a background of Christian culture that all our thought has significance," he declared. "An individual European may not believe the Christian faith is true; yet what he says and makes and does will all spring out of the heritage of Christian culture and depend upon that culture for a meaning." Thus Shelley, Byron, FitzGerald, Matthew Arnold, Huxley, Hardy, Darwin, Clifford, and hundreds more were all essentially "Anglican", either in action or reaction. "Only Christian society could produce a Voltaire or a Nietzsche: only Christian society could produce anti-Christians," Sweeney went on. Since there was no alternative to "The Vacant Mind" except a Christian civilization, he sought to redirect the thought of the English-speaking world towards the "Judaeo-Graeco-Catholic spiritual tradition."

Above all (and this is the keystone of his outlook) the saintly Sweeney has offered us the poetry and drama of purgation, damnation, and beatitude. He has exalted celibacy and the monastic state as the highest condition of mankind.

CHORUS

The lion and the unicorn,
    For sex once celebrated,
Are now bad-tempered and forlorn,
    For they have been castrated.

The bull Europa held so dear
    Is dead to all sensation,
Since he was turned into a steer
    By a simple operation.

The Gallic cock's triumphant crow
    No more shall greet the morrow,
A new-cut capon he lies low
    In meekness and in sorrow.

Those humans, too, have ceased to please
    Who moved us in "Orestes";
Electra's lost her ovaries
    And Strophius his testes.

The saintly Sweeney, your Holiness, has already in his lifetime become a legend. This, I submit, is no mere accident, but a spontaneous and almost universal tribute to his greatness. Even critics who dislike him are constrained to pay lip-service to his achievement. More than this, there has been a recognition of his essential *goodness* from every quarter of the Christian world, from every church and sect. That his virtue has been on the heroic level is vouched for in the cartloads of *litterae remissionales* which are waiting outside the door of the hall for your Holiness's inspection—should you wish to see them. I have no hesitation in saying that they present a complete case for my client's beatification. And, once beatified, and in due time translated into heaven, I, or my successor, will, I am convinced, be able to provide proof of countless miracles worked through his intercession which shall qualify him for enrolment in the Calendar of Saints.

THE "POPE"
I thank you, Mr X, for your eloquent address
Which will greatly help the Congregation to assess
The ratio of fancy and of fact
In Sweeney's legend, to sort "imagination all
   compact"
From what in vulgar phrase is "just an act",
To separate the cereal from the chaff,
And tell us when to cheer, to spit, or laugh.
I call upon the Devil's Advocate
To chalk his final debit on the slate.

DEVIL'S ADVOCATE
May it please your Holiness. With my learned friend's claims for his client as a critic I will summarily deal. That he should undertake a reassessment of the poets and their poems is signal proof of his courage: it is also, in view of some of his judgments, equal proof of his arrogance and foolhardiness. He elevates Dante above Shakespeare, as

my learned friend has told us, preferring the former's "divine intellectuality" to the latter's "muddled scepticism of the Renaissance". Since Dante slavishly adopted the thrice-muddled Aristotelianism of Aquinas as his philosophy, while Shakespeare's work is enriched by the great Renaissance humanists, this is more an admission of Sweeney's own limitations than an indication of Shakespeare's. A more trustworthy authority, Keats, says of Shakespeare, "How tremendous must have been his conception of Ultimates!" Goethe, says Sweeney (to put the finishing touch to his effrontery), "should not have attempted poetry at all, but should have confined himself to perfecting maxims, like La Rochefoucauld".

To dispose in detail of the Claimant's treatment of Milton would be to presume too much on the patience of the Court, but I will give one single instance to indicate its quality. He alleges that Milton is deficient in visual imagery and attributes it to the fact that he was blind. Even assuming that the charge were true (and there are scores of passages in his poems that would give it the lie), the fact is that Milton did not begin to go blind until he was thirty-six. Does not the Claimant believe that Milton could have remembered what he had seen sufficiently to revisualize it? Does he contend that Milton's "Paradise", because it is bounded only by aery vistas, is less actualized than Dante's "Inferno", which might well have been designed by the architect of Sing Sing or of the Empire State Building? Even Sweeney himself, in producing his own comparatively pale impressions of reality, did not always have the objects before his eyes as he wrote and must have relied on his memory. Homer, too, was blind, but Sweeney balks at denying *him* visual memory. Beethoven composed his greatest works long after he had gone deaf—but need I elaborate further, your Holiness?

The Claimant, incidentally, seems to cherish the illusion that publishing is a branch of literature. That some publishers who happened to be lovers of literature have in the past indulged their private tastes at the risk of their livelihood does not alter the fact that the *raison d'être* of publishing is to sell books—*any* books. Be this as it may, the growth in Britain of publishing "empires", inspired by transatlantic ideals, is depriving the Claimant's belief of all colourable excuse.

One difficulty in dealing with Sweeney is that when challenged on account of his opinions he has almost invariably modified them on his own principle of "obliquity" or, on occasions, when the game was becoming too hot, has entirely reversed his position. He is never more than a "fellow traveller" of reaction, and as such does not disdain protective colouring. Shakespeare, Milton, Burns, Shelley, and Blake will survive his belittlement—and Goethe, too: what is important to us is that Sweeney's standards are not primarily literary but theological.

Christian apologetics, as your Holiness should know better than anyone, is a science that can deal with *any* arguments. For example, statements of fact in Holy Writ remain statements of fact until they are proved otherwise; then they become "allegories". (The "Fifth Day" of Genesis, for example, in Auden becomes "Pleistocene Friday".) Similarly the crimes of the Church turn out to be crimes, not of the Church, but of the "age". Another favourite device of Christian apologists is to accuse their adversaries of using "obsolete" reason (e.g. logical positivism) to oppose the thoroughly "up-to-date" arguments of Aquinas[1] or Tertullian,[2] and still another is to attribute

[1] Including, presumably, those derived from the Neoplatonic forgery, the *Celestial Hierarchy* of the so-called Dionysius the Areopagite, which he took as the major basis for his "world order". Anti-Apologetics Department.

[2] *Quia absurdum*. Ditto.

to them opinions that they never held or expressed and then to demolish them—tricks as old as dishonesty itself, but effective with a semi-literate audience. But, as your Holiness will know, "God" is a political word, untranslatable into non-European languages, and has meaning only in a political context.

The "lovely Dante" (as Sweeney calls him) fully accepted the damnation of unbaptized infants. Sweeney confirms that they *are* damned, but owing presumably to his doctrinal commitments as a member of the Church of England, abstains from approving God's decision.

CHORUS
Original Sin, Original Sin,
Oh, what a terrible mess we are in!
Adam condemned the whole of his kin,
The young, the old, the fat, and the thin,
Even a saint like Augustín,
To suffer for ever the horrible in-
Iquity of Original Sin!

Freedom of Will, Freedom of Will,
Calvin's theology says it is nil,
That the ultimate fate of each Jack and each Jill
Is determined at birth for good or for ill,
But Sweeney, the orthodox, follows the drill
Like any Anglican run-of-the-mill,
Giving *one* cheer for Freedom of Will.

The Angelic Doctor (hailed as such by Sweeney) in his *De Unitate Intellectus Contra Averroistas*, condemned the proposition put forward by the civilized Arab, Averroes, that the human intellect is the same for the whole human race, as being blasphemous in the extreme. Speaking of

Aquinas with that understatement of which he is a past-master, Lord Russell says, "the finding of arguments for a conclusion given in advance is not philosophy, but special pleading." Like the Chesterbellocians, Sweeney harks back with nostalgia to the Middle Ages, not because he likes their spirit of equality in sin, but because he applauds their ignorance, their bigotry, their cruelty, and their dirt. A typical figure of the period was St Dominic, who hated learning like poison and who tore off the feathers of a living sparrow one by one, and then threw the bleeding carcase into the air.[1]

CHORUS
"The Christian has a special mind,
  Unlike the infidel or dog,"
Quoth Thomas, till the voice behind
  Of Averroes pierced the fog—
"The mind is one for all mankind,"
  He cried. Then *he* was just a wog!

That the Western is essentially a Christian civilization is the most oft-repeated of statements of orthodox apologetics—and the least true. The fact that the basic culture is vastly older than Christianity, with Graeco-Roman and countless other admixtures, has not prevented the official pundits from calling it "Judaeo-Christian". It follows that those who do not accept the Judaeo-Christian orthodoxy of the Establishment are not only "apostates" but cultural pariahs as well. If so, Western civilization will have to repudiate scores of great men who created those parts of it which are still alive and healthy.

[1] "Oh, but you omitted to mention that he thought it was the Devil!" Apologetics Department.
"We apologize. The learned Promotor also omitted Aquinas's remark that the contemplation of the agonies of the damned greatly enhanced the pleasures of the saved." Anti-Apologetics Department.

Only when Christianity is politically dead, that is to say as unorganized as Greek mythology, will its great imaginative resources be available to the poets. Sweeney himself admits that English religious poetry means "minor" poetry, and this is because of the anti-poetical associations of religion in our society. Thus he has to be "oblique" in order to be poetical, substituting Krishna for Christ and the *Upanishads* for the Scriptures.

Sweeney's contention that "only Christian society could produce anti-Christians" is tantamount to saying that only paganism could produce Christianity. His theory credits the piece of grit inside the oyster's shell with the creation of the pearl. We are asked to believe that just because Keats was not a Christian he wrote "Hyperion", that Shelley's "Prometheus Unbound" reflected the principles of Eldon and Castlereagh as in a distorting mirror, that the "Origin of Species" was the illegitimate offspring of Genesis, and such-like nonsense. The argument is good enough for apologetics but not, I submit, for your Holiness in Congregation.

As your Holiness is aware, this country is at present in the throes of a religious revival. Many who thought that "Reason" was a magic "open sesame" which had only to be uttered three times to solve all the problems of humanity, have been disillusioned. Thousands who marched out of the Churches a decade or two ago have now marched back. The aisles are choked with contrite agnostics and lapsed atheists. This has greatly encouraged the reactionaries. When, a year or two ago, Mrs Knight succeeded by some miracle in expressing some very mild rational opinions over the official air, she was met with a storm of howls and abuse which recalled Walpurgisnacht or the trial of the Salem witches.

Bury published his "History of the Freedom of

Thought" in 1913, but since then this freedom has declined to a mere fraction of what it was in the darkest days of Victoria's reign. Moreover, the religious "tests" have been silently reintroduced into many walks of life. All this, of course, has not been done under the threat of the brutal truncheon, but on the humane and praiseworthy principle that "one must respect other people's feelings." In practice, this means that I shall be assailed with religious propaganda of an intellectually and spiritually offensive nature through the mass media and otherwise be subjected to ecclesiastical pressure at all hours of the day without protection or redress, but that if I were to suggest ever so mildly that if Christianity were true it would be regrettable, I should forthwith be charged with causing a breach of the peace and most likely be deprived of my livelihood into the bargain. But persecution is the *sine qua non* of organized Christianity. Freedom of thought once progressed through the rivalry of the sects; the latter are now combining to satisfy their common urge to oppression. In America, Christianity is promoted on an undenominational basis, and "God" is advertised on huge placards in the railway-stations, without "brand", as if He were wool or tea.

The revival has been so successful and the pressures exercised so great that now every critic in Britain without exception belongs to the "Establishment", which, of course, as a political "front" is also undenominational. There are no rebels: they have all been won over or liquidated to the last man. However mildly condemnatory of Sweeney a critic may be, there is always a saving undercurrent of reverence for *what he stands for*. Indeed, in the literary weeklies, the languages of criticism and theology have become one and book reviews all sound like sermons written in the most holy "Double-Speak".

In such a situation it is easy to see how Sweeney as champion of the Judaeo-Christian revival has been carried to great heights by the tide. That he is, or originally was, a genuine poet is not contested by me, but I do assert that he has for altogether different reasons been "beatified" while still on earth. By a Congregation such as this, whose criteria are those of ethics, not of orthodoxy, I maintain that not only should Sweeney be refused beatification in our secular sense of the word, but that he should be excluded from the communion of Humaner Letters without the formality of bell, book, and candle.

THE "POPE"
>   Before I sum up on the evidence,
>   Taking account of legal precedents,
>   We'll hear what Mr Sweeney has to say,
>   Provided that he says it (a),
>   In words an Englishman can understand
>   Without a cipher-breaker in his hand,
>   And (b), provided that it's all
>   Unaided and original.
>   Claimant, speak up, we cannot see your face,
>   And let us hear you summarize your case.

THE VOICE OF SWEENEY
>   Because I do not want to think again
>   Because I do not want
>   Because I do not want to think
>   Desiring the blessed fame and saintly crown
>   I no longer want to want what you would want me want
>   (Why should the baptized infant want the font?)
>   Why should I plead
>   To gentiles branded with the mark of Cain?

DEVIL'S ADVOCATE
    He means, your Holiness, that he denies the jurisdiction of the Court.

THE "POPE"
    Just as I thought.

THE VOICE OF SWEENEY
    The abomination of desolation
That is literal thinking—Gibbon, Hume, and Newton,
And, in our time, Russell and Bishop Barnes,
Darwin, too, and the superficial notion of evolution,
In the popular mind a means of disowning the past,
Secular impertinence, card-index revelation,
Born of midnight oil,
Human self-sufficiency,
Trial and error, and mathematical induction,
Nonsensical beside the transcendental genesis of the
    Upanishads
That the universe began as *Brahmānda*,
A soft-boiled egg,
Without salt or pepper,
(A conception repeated in the Orphic legend),
Or even that of an Ouspensky,
A latter-day Ezekiel,
That the moon is a younger earth,
The earth a younger sun,
And that the planetary bodies are living things,
(Just as Professor Challenger said they were,
And, to prove it,
Pricked the earth through its crust with an electric-
    drill
So that it projected a column of stinking fluid
Right into his eye

Like an enormous and exasperated sea-urchin),
Which leads to "self-remembering",
Then to "occult reflection",
After that to "intellectual anti-thinking",
And finally to "objective unconsciousness",
An experience so ecstatic
That it makes a good dinner
Seem like a bad one.
(I sometimes wonder whether this is what Krishna
   meant).
Abomination, too, of humanistic sentiment,
Insufflation of vile bodies
And viler personalities,
Airy-fairy "sweetness and light".
As to the unbridled licence,
The blasphemous incontinence,
Permitted by the BBC
To that rationalistic Jezebel,
That impious disbeliever, Mrs X,
Not only were we displeased,
Hurt, pained, grieved, and disappointed,
But, what is more,
We were *not* amused!

CHORUS
A public Corporation stands accused,
Its hospitality has been abused,
A precious privilege has been misused,
And Faith (already sick) lies badly bruised,
And hence (quite naturally) the Saintly One
   is *not* amused!

ECHO
Not *amused—mused.*

THE VOICE OF SWEENEY

    Flitting between the dimness and the dark
Blessed the dim-eyed bat; blasphemous the lark
This lingering illness, fitful fever, "living"
Help me, Jesus, though I do not want to want these
    things
From the airless dungeon towards the breathless shore
Wings that are suffocating, coma-giving
Angelic wings. . . . .

THE "POPE"

      If this were an actual Papal court and not the
                          figment of a dream,
It's more than probable that I, as Pontifex, would
    deem
That Mr Sweeney had made good his claim
To blessedness through universal fame
Of virtue practised in heroical degree,
And that subject to the rule of Holy See
Which calls for miracles encompassed by
The blessed's intervention when on high,
He'd in due season take his lofty seat
Beneath the Father, Son, and Paraclete.
He's orthodox, his tenets are as strict
As those of Xavier or of Benedict,
And as for chastity, his views recall
The famous admonition of St Paul.

But we, a court of men, have other tests—
Whether or not the Claimant manifests
A talent for credulity or revels
In lice, or fasts, or fisticuffs with devils,
Is quite irrelevant. We do not care
Whether he's nude or wears a shirt of hair

Or, like St Simeon, lives up in the air.
We proffer questions of a different grain—
Whether he's enlightened or humane,
How would he pleasure a wench or drive a spigot?
Is he of tolerant mind or just a bigot?
Has he the zest for life of Rabelais
(Accepting, of course, the standards of our day)?
Is he as joyous as Boccaccio?
In both these cases we must answer "No".
Would Falstaff choose him as a drinking pal?
How would he fare with Bardolph or Prince Hal?
Has he the quiet detachment of Montaigne?
Can he compete with Milton's epic strain?
Would Dryden praise his satire, or would Pope
Approve his riddles or his narrow scope?
Has he a touch of Browning's lyric gift,
Or *saeva indignatio* of Swift?
Has Blake's compassion taught his heart to sing?
Has he the lift of Shelley's heavenly wing?
Has he the humour that would save his feet
From falling in the pitfalls of conceit
Waiting to trap the clerical élite?

My Lordships, acting Cardinals, I hear your shouts
   of "No!"
And, truth to tell, I knew it must be so,
And since there's nothing left for me to say
I'll give my judgment with no more delay.
Loyola Sweeney! Ushers, repeat his name.

USHERS

Loyola Sweeney!
Despite your widespread sacerdotal fame,

Your minor poet's laurels, your monkish living free
   from active blame,
This Congregation disallows your claim.

THE VOICE OF SWEENEY
     Between the mystification
     And the deception
     Between the multiplication
     And the division
     Falls the Tower of London.

     Many Nouns in *is* we find
     To the Masculine assigned:
     Amnis, axis, caulis, collis,
     Clunis, crinis, fascis, follis...
     Take away the number you first thought of...[1]
     Stop breeding...
     Stop breathing...
         Pop!

USHER
He has kicked the bucket, your Holiness!

         CHORUS
     This is the way that Sweeney ends
     This is the way that Sweeney ends
     This is the way that Sweeney ends
     Not with a curse but a mutter
     Not with a flight but a flutter
     Not with a song but a stutter.

---

[1] "Only mustard isn't a bird," Alice remarked. "Right as usual," said the Duchess: "what a clear way you have of putting things!"

III
THE AWAKENING

Then I woke up! It was all, of course, a dream,
Just my long repressed libido letting off some steam.
But though it has a lot of gaps and is sometimes queer in its chronology,
It's a pretty fair impression of an average anthology.
Yet Sweeney isn't dead, they say, his ticker's still aloofly ticking;
He's theoretically alive, though not exactly kicking.
(Extant and sniffing, that would be the better phrase,
Which incidentally well describes the tempo of his plays).

But what has happened to Letters, with Sweeney as High Critic?
The answer is, his followers have brought the system analytic
To the acme of perfection. A poem is now "placed"
Within the Great Tradition, its pedigree is traced
Like that of bloodstock, and biographic chit-chat is effaced.
They tell a well-bred lyric by its whinnies,
And prove that its grandsire won the Thousand Guineas.
The verdict nowadays is absolute
And one that none dare challenge or refute,
For, unlike all other man-made things, Analysis
Is free from human jealousies and malices
And quite devoid of formal fallacies,
And since a modern poem is a rigorous totality,
Emancipated from "originality",

The product of a highly specialized technique
Of which the hierophants alone can speak
By virtue of their rubrics, amended once a week
And issued secretly in Hittite and in Greek,
A process academic, sacerdotal, esoteric,
It follows that each practitioner must be a *cleric*.
Indeed, the whole Establishment—poets, critics,
    publishers, worker-bees, and warders,
Are all of them at least in minor orders.
Theirs is a Church (though when the infidels attack it
They call it just a "mournful little racket").
You either buy the products of their trade
Or read the poems you yourself have made.
To say which evil is the lesser of the two
I fear I must, dear reader, leave to you.

So, what is a girl to do?

When all is said and done, there *is* a "Vacant Mind",
Even if it isn't of the kind
That Sweeney's holy nightmare claimed to find.
The poetry that expressed our national reality,
The essence of autochthonous vitality,
That reconciled the aims of mass and personality,
The vehicle of joy, or beauty, or of rage,
A limpid distillation of the spirit of the age,
Melodious epitome of our island heritage,
Has dwindled to a psalmody of clerical fanatics,
As far away from common life as Higher Mathematics,
And vanished are the poets who used to live in attics.
All this has left a vacuum, a crepitating void,
That can't be filled by Billy Graham, mescaline, jazz,
    breathing-exercises, Emily Post, or even Freud,
And since it's true that Rhythm is to Time as Symmetry
    to Space,

We British have become an inharmonious race
Of tone-deaf "hearties" or exporting beavers,
Debilitated pagans or certified "believers",
Playing a horrid dirge on marrow-bones and cleavers.

But if it wasn't always thus,
When did we take the wrong direction; when did we
   "miss the bus"?

According to *my* theory of "catastrophe",
The answer to this question's plain enough to see—
It happened in the twenties of last century,
When, with the passing of the Immortal Three,
The beacon-fire of Universal Poesy
Went out, and in its stead
The only lights to show the way ahead
Were patriotic lanterns—yellow, green, or red—
Of Poets Laureate, or else the wicked gleam
Of Conquest's *ignis fatuus*, or Greed's ignoble beam.
Meanwhile a man could hardly see to read
By the farthing rush-light of the Established Creed,
And Architecture could not breathe the air
Of Evangelic, Neo-Gothic Laissez-faire.
The realm was now a nigger-drivers' stud-yard,
And cradle for the coming mud-and-blood-yard
Of Empire, whose prophet was the celebrated Rudyard.
At length the rule of Critics and decline of taste
Resulted in the present howling waste.

And where do we come in as mere consumers,
If none will pay attention to our humours?
The Reverend Practitioners,
They cater solely for communicant parishioners,
Despite the ancient principle,
The fixed contractual rule,

From which the craft of poetry is not immune,
That, "He who pays the piper calls the tune,"
And since the clerics offer no solution
But merely bolster up their rotten institution,
Come, boys and girls, we'll stage a REVOLUTION!

PEOPLE'S CHORUS

    Let a vast assembly be
    And with great solemnity
    Declare with measured words that we
    Will fashion our own poetry.

    And with solemn words make known
    Henceforth we utterly disown
    Tracts in verse and drama bleak,
    Coinage of a tyrant clique.

    Proclaim to all our common will
    To live this life unto its fill,
    The while to smite both thigh and hip
    The cult of Anti-Lifemanship.

    Sternly the false pretence reject
    That poets are a chosen sect—
    Despite their superhuman powers,
    Shakespeare, Milton, Keats are *ours*!

    There rides Sweeney on his way,
    Mounted on a gelding grey,
    Very smooth he looks yet grim;
    Seven tomcats follow him.

    Next there comes an ebon hearse,
    Piléd high with Sweeney's verse;
    In the driver's face are seen
    The features of the Gloomy Dean.

Following this on foot there pass,
With frozen mien and eyes of glass,
Beneath a flock of circling kites,
A troop of Sweeney's acolytes.

And last there comes Authority,
Preceded by his lictors three,
Assailing us with rasping cry—
"*Yours* is not to reason why!
Obey your God; your God is *I*!"

The night is black, but now we hear
The strain of strutting Chanticleer;
Dissolved in light the spectres fade,
Ending the ghastly masquerade.

Now hear us, heavenly Harmony,
And eke thy sister, Melody,
So long as exiled prisoners pent,
Return to us from banishment.

Let a vast assembly be
And with great solemnity
Declare with measured words that we
Will fashion our own poetry.

Rise like songbirds after slumber
In unvanquishable number,
The sweetness of our tongue renew,
Drive the ravens from the blue,
Ye are many—they are few!

BIBLIOGRAPHY

WRITINGS BY T. S. ELIOT REFERRED TO IN THE INTRODUCTION

All references to the poems and plays may be found in *The Complete Poems and Plays*, London, 1969. References to the *Selected Essays* below are to the third edition, London, 1951.

1917 'Ezra Pound: his Metric and Poetry', in *To Criticise the Critic*, London, 1965.
1917 'Reflections on *Vers Libre*', in *To Criticise the Critic*, London, 1965.
1919 'The Method of Mr Pound'; *Athenaeum*, 24 October, London.
1919 'Tradition and the Individual Talent' in *Selected Essays*.
1920 *The Sacred Wood*, London, second edition, 1928.
1921 'The Metaphysical Poets', in *Selected Essays*.
1921 'Andrew Marvell', in *Selected Essays*.
1923 'The Function of Criticism', in *Selected Essays*.
1927 'Shakespeare and the Stoicism of Seneca', in *Selected Essays*.
1927 'Baudelaire', in *Selected Essays*.
1928 *For Lancelot Andrewes*, London.
1928 'The Humanism of Irving Babbitt', in *Selected Essays*.
1928 'Isolated Superiority', *Dial*, LXXXIV, no. 1, New York.
1929 'Second Thoughts on Humanism', in *Selected Essays*.
1929 'Dante', in *Selected Essays*.
1930 Introduction to Johnson's *London*, London.
1930 Introduction to *Anabasis*, by St John Perse, London.
1931 'Thoughts after Lambeth', in *Selected Essays*.
1933 *The Use of Poetry and the Use of Criticism*, London.
1934 *After Strange Gods*, London.
1935 Introduction to *Selected Poems of Marianne Moore*, London.
1935 'Religion and Literature', in *Selected Essays*.
1936 *Essays Ancient and Modern*, London.
1937 untitled essay in *Revelation*, ed. Baillie and Martin, London.
1939 *The Idea of a Christian Society*, London.
1940 'Yeats', in *On Poetry and Poets*, London, 1957.
1941 Introduction to *A Choice of Kipling's Verse*, London.
1942 'The Music of Poetry', in *On Poetry and Poets*, London, 1957.

1942 'The Classics and the Man of Letters', in *To Criticise the Critic*, London, 1965.
1948 *Notes towards a Definition of Culture*, London.
1950 'What Dante means to me', in *To Criticise the Critic*, London, 1965.
1951 *Selected Essays*, third edition (first edition 1932), London.
1956 'Frontiers of Criticism', in *On Poetry and Poets*, London, 1957.
1957 *On Poetry and Poets*, London.
1965 *To Criticise the Critic*, London.
1971 'The Waste Land'; a facsimile and transcript, ed. V. Eliot, London.

WORKS ON T. S. ELIOT REFERRED TO IN THE INTRODUCTION

Aiken, C., *New Republic*, vol. 33, New York, 1923.
Baillie, J., and Martin, H. (eds), *Revelation*, London, 1937.
Bateson, F. W., *Essays in Critical Dissent*, London, 1972.
Bateson, F. W., 'Criticism's Lost Leader' (see Molina).
Bullough, G., *Mirror of Minds*, London, 1962.
Craig, D., 'The defeatism of "The Waste Land" ', *Critical Quarterly*, vol. 2, 1960.
Daiches, D., *The Present Age: after 1920*, London, 1958.
Davie, D., 'Anglican Eliot' (see Litz).
Fabricius, J., *The Unconscious and Mr. Eliot*, Copenhagen, 1958.
Forster, E. M., *Abinger Harvest*, London, 1936.
Frank, J., 'Spatial Form in Modern Literature', *Sewanee Review*, no. 53, 1945.
Gardner, H., *The Art of T. S. Eliot*, London, 1949/68.
Gardener, H., 'Four Quartets' (see Rajan).
Hay, E. K., *T. S. Eliot's Negative Way*, Harvard, 1982.
Hopkins, K., *A Dull Head among Windy Spaces*, North Walsham, 1976.
Hough, G., *Image and Experience*, London, 1960.
Kenner, H., 'The urban apocalyse' (see Litz).
Langbaum, R., 'New modes of characterization in "The Waste Land" ' (see Litz).
Laski, H., *Faith, Reason and Civilization*, New York, 1944.
Leavis, F. R., *New Bearings in English Poetry*, London, 1932.
Leavis, F. R., *English Literature in our Time*, London, 1969.

Lewis, W., *Men without Art*, London, 1934.
Litz, A. W. (ed.), *Eliot in his Time*, London, 1973.
Mangan, S., 'A Note: on the Somewhat Premature Apotheosis of T. S. Eliot' *Pagany*, Spring no., New York, 1930.
Martin, G. (ed.), *Eliot in Perspective*, London, 1970.
Matthiessen, F. O., *The Achievement of T. S. Eliot*, New York, 1935/59.
Molina, D. N. de (ed.), *The Literary Criticism of T. S. Eliot*, London, 1977.
Moody, A. D., *T. S. Eliot, poet*, Cambridge, 1979.
Rajan, B. (ed.), *T. S. Eliot*, London, 1947.
Read, H., *The Psychopathology of Reaction in the Arts*, ICA, London, 1955.
Richards, I. A., *Principles of Literary Criticism*, London, 1924/26.
Robbins, R. H., *The T. S. Eliot Myth*, New York, 1951.
Ross Williamson, H., *The Poetry of T. S. Eliot*, London, 1932.
Simmons, J., *No Land is Waste, Dr. Eliot*, London, 1972.
Smith, G., *The Waste Land*, London, 1983.
Spender, S., *The Destructive Element*, London, 1935.
Spender, S., *Eliot*, London, 1975.
Traversi, D., *T. S. Eliot: the longer poems*, London, 1976
Untermeyer, L., *Freeman*, vol. 6, New York, 1923.
Wheelwright, P., 'Eliot's Philosophical Themes' (see Rajan).
Wilson, E., *Dial*, no. 73, New York, 1922.
Wilson, E., *Axel's Castle*, New York, 1931.
Wilson, E., 'Miss Buttle and Mr. Eliot', *New Yorker*, XXIV, no. 14, New York, 1958.
Winters, Y., *Primitivism and Decadence*, New York, 1937.
Winters, Y., *The Anatomy of Nonsense*, Norfolk, Conn., 1943.
Yeats, W. B., Introduction to *The Oxford Book of Modern Verse*, Oxford, 1936.